Preface

The Air Force is committed to eliminating sexual assault in the service. It is therefore considering how its policies and procedures for screening at enlistment might help prevent sexual assault. This report reviews current Air Force recruitment and enlistment policies and procedures and assesses how these may reduce sexual assault perpetration. It also reviews the strengths and limitations of self-report tests that may be used to predict counterproductive workplace behaviors and considers the applicability of these and other assessments, including background checks and personality assessments, to sexual assault prevention. The report concludes by providing preliminary recommendations for the Air Force to consider as part of its efforts to prevent sexual assault in the service.

The research reported here was sponsored by the Director of Air Force Sexual Assault Prevention and Response, Office of the Vice Chief of Staff, and the commander of Air Force Recruiting Service. It was conducted within the Manpower, Personnel, and Training Program of RAND Project AIR FORCE as part of a fiscal year 2014 study, "Enhancing Sexual Assault Prevention and Response Efforts Through a Better Understanding of Perpetrator Behaviors and Risk Factors."

RAND Project AIR FORCE

RAND Project AIR FORCE (PAF), a division of the RAND Corporation, is the U.S. Air Force's federally funded research and development center for studies and analyses. PAF provides the Air Force with independent analyses of policy alternatives affecting the development, employment, combat readiness, and support of current and future aerospace forces. Research is conducted in four programs: Force Modernization and Employment; Manpower, Personnel, and Training; Resource Management; and Strategy and Doctrine. The research reported here was prepared under contract FA7014-06-C-0001.

Additional information about PAF is available on our website:
http://www.rand.org/paf

Contents

Assessing the Use of Employment Screening for Sexual Assault Prevention

Miriam Matthews

RAND Project AIR FORCE

Prepared for the United States Air Force
Approved for public release; distribution unlimited

For more information on this publication, visit www.rand.org/t/RR1250

Library of Congress Cataloging-in-Publication Data is available for this publication.

ISBN: 978-0-8330-9200-7

Published by the RAND Corporation, Santa Monica, Calif.

© Copyright 2017 RAND Corporation

RAND® is a registered trademark.

Support RAND
Make a tax-deductible charitable contribution at
www.rand.org/giving/contribute

www.rand.org

Figures and Tables

Figures

Tables

Summary

Recent estimates show that 2.90 percent of active-duty women and 0.29 percent of active-duty men in the U.S. Air Force experienced a sexual assault in the past year (Jaycox et al., 2015). Such experiences can have long-term physical and psychological consequences for victims, including gynecological complications and depression (Jewkes, Sen, and Garcia-Moreno, 2002). The threat of sexual assault can also decrease self-perceptions and trust in others (Bohner and Schwartz, 1996).

The Air Force is committed to preventing sexual assault among its members. As part of its effort to do so, it asked RAND to examine how the Air Force might modify current policies and procedures to identify potential recruits at risk of perpetrating sexual assault. This report reviews current efforts during recruitment to address sexual assault prevention and the policies and practices the Air Force may wish to adopt for screening recruits.

For this research, the RAND project team held discussions with representatives from the U.S. Air Force Recruiting Service (AFRS) and individuals who facilitate the screening process at the Military Entrance Processing Station (MEPS). The team spoke with these individuals about general recruitment and accession processes for enlisted airmen, as well as about information recruits receive regarding sexual assault or sexual-harassment policies in the Air Force. The team also reviewed employment-screening measures, such as integrity tests, background assessments, and personality assessments, used to predict and address negative workplace behaviors and examined whether these measures may be used to identify prospective applicants with a proclivity to commit sexual harassment or sexual assault. While no single best method for screening such recruits emerged, there are some practices the Air Force may consider.

Addressing Sexual Assault Prevention in Air Force Recruitment

The Air Force has several opportunities to find and address potentially problematic behavior that might be used to screen recruits and to convey information about norms of appropriate behavior. The service's Intervene, Dissuade, Deter, Detect, and Accountability program holds recruiters responsible for communicating the guidelines for appropriate recruiter-applicant interactions prior to an applicant's initial processing at a MEPS. Recruiters also must review and require applicants to acknowledge Air Force policy on discrimination and sexual harassment (see HQ AFRS, 2013), and must provide each recruit with information that outlines the fundamental aspects of becoming a professional airman.

After an individual expresses interest in the Air Force, a recruiter will typically review several prequalification criteria with the applicant. Such a preliminary assessment includes review of applicants' prior behavior. Whether an individual is explicitly asked about a history of behavior related to sexual assault, including aggressive or violent behavior, can vary by the topics a recruiter thinks most important.

For all applicants, recruiters complete Directives Division (DD) Form 2807-2, Accessions Medical Prescreen Report, which addresses mental-health conditions that may disqualify an applicant. Persons with potentially disqualifying answers (e.g., a history of psychological counseling) require additional documentation to be considered further. Recruits who proceed further in their application must complete the Standard Form 86, Questionnaire for National Security Positions, which the military services and others use as part of the application for a security clearance. Applicants must also undergo a background check to receive a security clearance. These forms and background checks may uncover potentially disqualifying offenses, for which applicants must also receive waivers for further consideration. More-severe offenses (e.g., rape, aggravated assault with a deadly weapon) require waivers from higher authorities and are given far less frequently than those for less-severe offenses.[1]

Applicants who advance to a Military Entry Processing Command appointment receive a physical exam and several other assessments. Recently, the Air Force has begun to administer the Tailored Adaptive Personality Assessment System (TAPAS), which assesses applicant personality. Several personality dimensions TAPAS assesses may be associated with proclivity to perpetrate sexual assault, but research has not yet assessed these associations. Although currently given to all applicants, TAPAS is only operational as a point of information for selection into some positions, which include battlefield airman and related Air Force specialties. Other Military Entry Processing Command forms ask about medical history and past behaviors, including alcohol and drug abuse, that may be associated with sexual assault perpetration but do not ask specifically about the applicant's prior sexual history and history of sexual assault or about accusations of sexual assault made against the applicant.

Applicability of Various Measures for Sexual Assault Prevention

Many organizations have introduced various measures, including background checks, integrity tests, and personality assessments, to screen their applicants for undesirable potential workplace behaviors, including theft, absenteeism, and violence. Such measures have became increasingly popular since the effective prohibition of polygraph examinations for U.S. businesses.[2] These tests are usually administered by paper and pencil or by computer to participants.

---

[1] Waivers for severe offenses are provided for situations that are highly specific to each applicant. For example, a waiver for rape may be considered if an applicant engaged in sexual intercourse at the age of 18 with a willing partner who was the age of 17. This is considered statutory rape in some, but not all, states. A commanding officer may review the circumstances of such a case to determine whether a moral waiver may be warranted.

[2] Polygraph examinations are still allowed in the U.S. federal government.

Integrity tests are some of the most well-known employment screening measures. Integrity tests may be overt, directly assessing attitudes toward counterproductive thoughts and actions (e.g., theft, drug use), or personality-based, measuring personality dimensions that may predict counterproductive behaviors (e.g., low conscientiousness). Researchers have found substantial differences between these tests and the constructs they are designed to address. For example, one meta-analysis found the average validity coefficient, or association, between integrity tests and job performance to be strong, at 0.41 (Ones, Viswesvaran, and Schmidt, 1993), whereas a later meta-analysis found the average validity coefficient between these tests and job performance to be weaker, at below 0.20 (Van Iddekinge et al., 2012). Observed differences in the strength of validity coefficients may be due to differences across the designs of meta-analyses, including differential consideration of studies conducted by those who are and those who are not responsible for publishing (and selling) the assessments and differences in consideration of the methodological rigor of studies.

The ability of integrity tests to predict behaviors may also vary by measurement method, the breadth of a measure (e.g., whether it is for a specific behavior or a more-general trait), and the group that is tested. For example, one meta-analysis found stronger associations between integrity tests and self-admissions of behavior than between these tests and supervisory ratings (Ones, Viswesvaran, and Schmidt, 1993). This meta-analysis also found stronger associations between integrity tests and theft criteria than between these tests and other disruptive behaviors and found larger validities between integrity tests and counterproductive workplace behaviors for incumbent samples than for applicant samples.

Effective use of integrity tests requires addressing several challenges. Tests may be vulnerable both to test-taker deception and to misclassification of employees. Misclassification is particularly problematic when attempting to predict behaviors that occur relatively infrequently. To guard against misclassification, organizations may wish to use these tests and other screening measures only when applicants are shown to have an extremely high proclivity to commit an infrequent behavior. This may be part of a multiphase screening procedure. Alternatively, organizations may use integrity tests and other screening measures for particular positions in selecting among individuals already employed.

Although used to predict negative workplace behaviors, such as theft, substance use, and absenteeism, integrity tests have not been used to screen for proclivity to commit sexual assault. Before using such measures to predict sexual assault proclivity, the Air Force would need to assess test validity among those on whom the tests would be used, such as current enlistees or recruits. In addition, validation studies can assess criterion-related validity, that is, whether there is an association between the measure and the outcome interest. Studies of criterion-related validity may use predictive methodology, involving data collection at different times, or concurrent methodology, involving data collection at the same time. Although no assessment is without limitations (e.g., see Hall, 1990), criterion-related validity assessments that may be considered include prospective studies involving Air Force personnel or applicants (e.g.,

Thompson et al., 2011) and longitudinal studies involving Air Force personnel or applicants (e.g., Abbey and McAuslan, 2004). Another criterion-related validity assessment that may be considered is examination of the association between the responses of Air Force applicants or personnel to these measures and their responses on previous sexual assault behavior or on the extent to which they would conduct sexual assault if there were no chance of being caught (e.g., Drieschner and Lange, 1999).

Additional assessments may also consider content validity—the extent to which a test measures the construct of interest—using, for example, comparisons between the responses of those convicted for sexual assault in the Air Force and the responses of a random sample of Air Force personnel or applicants (e.g., Malamuth, 1981). These two groups have differences in their proclivity toward conduct sexual assault. Differences in their responses to a measure of sexual assault proclivity differ would suggest that the measure is assessing the construct of interest. The Air Force should also assess the extent to which these measures may lead to misclassification, such as incorrectly classifying individuals as prone to commit a behavior that they would not commit (i.e., false positives) or not prone to commit a behavior that they would commit (i.e., false negatives) (e.g., National Research Council, 2003).

Beyond integrity tests, other measures seek to assess respondent levels of sexual aggression and likelihood to commit sexual assault, but the predictive validity of these measures has not been established (for additional information, see Greathouse et al., 2015). The Air Force may therefore wish to use such measures as antisocial personality characteristics or desire to sexually dominate a victim as but one point of information in a selection system for positions requiring extensive interaction with subordinates, such as trainer or recruiter, making those with higher scores less likely to be selected for such positions.

Conclusions and Recommendations

This review points to several recommendations that may assist the Air Force in addressing and communicating to applicants the service's lack of tolerance for sexual assault. There are several points during a person's career at which the Air Force may implement sexual assault prevention efforts.

First, when providing applicants with information on professional and unprofessional behaviors in the service, the Air Force should provide thorough information about its intolerance of sexual assault.[3] By presenting information early in the application process, the service can quickly begin a sustained prevention effort that clearly communicates the service's attitude and response toward sexual assault. At the same time, the Air Force should evaluate the effect of

---

[3] Prevention is broader than education and attitude change. For example, it may also include other behavioral interventions, such as for alcohol consumption (Abbey, McAuslan, and Ross, 1998 et al.; Farris and Heppner, 2014).

providing this information, including assessment of knowledge and attitudes immediately after provision and subsequent repeated measurement of behaviors.

Second, the Air Force should obtain more information about an applicant's behavioral history early in the application process. During the prescreening and preapplication of applicants, the Air Force should ask applicants about whether they have a history of sexual assault perpetration. Alternatively, the MEPS may conduct standardized assessments that address this behavior. Previous sexual assault behavior is the best available predictor of future such behavior. Asking for this information further communicates to applicants the Air Force's commitment to addressing sexual assault. The Air Force should also pretest such assessments to determine their impact on applicant perceptions of and inclinations to join the Air Force. Individuals may omit information from self-reports, so the Air Force may consider more-thorough background checks that specifically assess an individual's history of sexual assault. Assessing prior sexual assault behavior as part of a more thorough background check, such as during an investigation for national security clearance, would require coordination with federal entities. Alternatively, the Air Force could fund and coordinate its own additional background check. Both options would require extensive time and resources and should be pursued only with the approval of appropriate parties, including legal entities, and after pretesting applicants or potential applicants to the Air Force.

Third, given that no employment-screening measure clearly related to likelihood of sexual assault perpetration currently exists, the Air Force could consider use of other measures somewhat associated with proclivity for such behavior. For example, TAPAS addresses such dimensions as consideration for others, cooperation, self-control, responsibility, nondelinquency, virtue, and even-temperedness that may be useful for the Air Force to consider or review (Stark et al., 2014). Developing its own compatibility tool for screening applicants would require the Air Force to devote resources, including time, to creating and testing the validity of the measure. The Air Force Personnel Center began development and initial validity assessment of screening measures for sexual assault in fiscal year 2014. The Air Force needs to validate these tests with the population to which they will be administered (e.g., applicants) and to examine the extent to which they may misclassify individuals. Researchers should also assess the extent to which these measures can withstand potential legal, privacy, and fairness challenges. Scores on such measures could be particularly helpful in evaluating a person's suitability relative to others for such Air Force positions as recruiter or trainer or for other positions that frequently interact with subordinates.

If these actions are taken and effective, reported sexual assault in the Air Force, such as anonymous reports of sexual assault (e.g., Morral, Gore, and Schell, 2014), should decrease.[4] In

_____

[4] Notably, anonymous reports serve as one potential source of information, and additional information, including climate perceptions and commander feedback, may also assist with assessment of efficacy.

sum, by making some changes to current policies and practices, the Air Force may further improve its sexual assault prevention efforts.

Acknowledgments

I would first like to thank the project sponsors for their support and guidance throughout this work. In the Air Force Sexual Assault Prevention and Response (SAPR) in the Office of the Vice Chief of Staff (AV/CVS), the project began under the sponsorship of Maj Gen Margaret Woodward and was then completed under the guidance of Lt Gen Gina Grosso. In the Air Force Recruiting Service (AFRS), the project began under the sponsorship of Maj Gen John Horner and was then completed under the guidance of Maj Gen James Johnson.

I also wish to thank those at AFRS who provided input on this project, including Angelo Haygood, Hector Acosta, and SMSgt Pedro Colon, and those at the San Antonio Military Entrance Processing Station who provided information to and participated in discussions with RAND. In addition, Courtney Knoth and Andra Tharp of SAPR and Laura Barron of the Air Force Personnel Center provided helpful comments. From RAND, Kirsten Keller assisted with interviews and other discussions and provided thoughtful comments and suggestions. Laura Miller, Sarah Greathouse, and Jessica Saunders of RAND offered helpful comments on the report. Carra Sims and Maria Lytell reviewed previous drafts. I also thank Susan Straus and Paul Sackett for their thorough formal reviews and helpful comments.

Abbreviations

AETC	Air Education and Training Command
AFRS	Air Force Recruiting Service
ASVAB	Armed Services Vocational Aptitude Battery
BMT	basic military training
CCMAPPEDDS	citizenship, conscientious objector, morals, age, prior service, physical, education, drugs, dependents, and social security
CMO	chief medical officer
CRT-A	Conditional Reasoning Test for Aggression
DD	Directives Division
DEP	Delayed Entry Program
FY	fiscal year
ID3A	Intervene, Dissuade, Deter, Detect, and Accountability
LNCO	liaison noncommissioned officers
MEPS	Military Entrance Processing Station
MOS	military occupational specialty
NPS	non–prior service
NRC	National Research Council
OSD	Office of the Secretary of Defense
OTA	Office of Technology Assessment
SF	standard form
SG	surgeon general
TAPAS	Tailored Adaptive Personality Assessment System
UCMJ	Universal Code of Military Justice
UIF	unfavorable information files
USMEPCOM	U.S. Military Entry Processing Command

1. Introduction

Recent estimates show that 2.90 percent of active-duty women and 0.29 percent of active-duty men in the U.S. Air Force had experienced a sexual assault in the past year (Jaycox et al., 2015). The experience of sexual assault can have long-term physical and psychological consequences for victims, including gynecological complications and depression (Jewkes, Sen, and Garcia-Moreno, 2002). The threat of sexual assault can decrease self-perceptions and trust in others (Bohner and Schwartz, 1996).

The Air Force is committed to preventing sexual assault among its service members. As part of its prevention efforts, the service supported the research reported here into how it could modify its current policies and procedures to identify potential recruits who may have an increased risk of perpetrating sexual assault. Although the focus of this research is on new recruits, RAND also considered policies and procedures involved with the selection of airmen into particular positions in the Air Force.

Throughout, this report draws from the Universal Code of Military Justice (UCMJ) to define sexual assault. Article 120 of the UCMJ defines four offenses considered to constitute a broad category of sexual assault: rape, sexual assault, aggravated sexual contact, and abusive sexual contact. In addition, Article 80 of the UCMJ addresses attempts to conduct certain offenses, including those described in Article 120.

Sexual Assault Screening Tools

Previous RAND work (Greathouse et al., 2015) described several complex influences on sexual assault perpetration and multiple reasons an individual might commit sexual assault. that work concluded that there is no single profile for a sexual assault perpetrator and that different combinations of factors likely influence perpetration. As a result, it is difficult to predict whether any one individual is likely to commit sexual assault in the future.

Nevertheless, Greathouse et al. (2015) noted that several measures are associated with a respondent's likelihood of committing sexual assault. Many of these address gender-related attitudes and cognitions. For example, some research has shown an association between responses to rape-myth acceptance scales (e.g., "When women talk and act sexy, they are inviting rape"), which address misperceived justification of rape and of sexual assault perpetration (Carr and VanDeusen, 2004; Zawacki et al., 2003). Research with civilian samples has also shown an association between responses to measures of hostility toward women (e.g., "Sometimes women bother me by just being around") and sexual assault perpetration (Abbey and McAuslan, 2004; Hall et al., 2000). Other attitudinal measures that appear to be somewhat associated with sexual assault perpetration include beliefs in traditional gender roles (e.g., "It is ridiculous for a woman to run a train and a man to sew clothes" [Abbey, McAuslan, and Ross, 1998]) and hypermasculinity or hostile masculinity (e.g., "I know feminists want to be like men because men are better than women" [Malamuth et al., 1995]).

Measures of peer attitudes and behaviors have also shown associations with measures of sexual assault perpetration. For example, those who perceive that their peers approve of sexual assault appear to be somewhat more likely to commit sexual assault (Capaldi et al., 2001). Similarly, those who perceive that their peers are sexually aggressive are more likely to perpetrate sexual assault (DeKeseredy and Kelly, 1995).

Other factors that appear associated with sexual assault perpetration include alcohol use and drug use (Swartout and White, 2010; Zawacki et al., 2003). Various interpersonal-skill deficits have shown mixed associations with sexual assault proclivity (e.g., Baker and Beech, 2004; Fernandez and Marshall, 2003). Finally, past perpetration of sexual assault is one of the most consistent predictors of future perpetration (Loh et al., 2005; Zinzow and Thompson, 2015).

Importantly, research on measures of the previously described constructs and sexual assault behaviors tends to show weak associations, mixed effects, or effects that are conditional on certain contexts or constructs (see Greathouse et al., 2015). None of these studies have been designed to prospectively predict future sexual assault. No survey measure, preemployment screening test, or checklist has yet been developed to predict sexual aggression that consistently and strongly predicts sexual assault behaviors or sexual assault proclivity among nonadjudicated samples. Thus, a self-report instrument that may be used to identify individuals as being at high risk of perpetrating sexual assault has not yet been developed. That said, research has considered predictors of sexual aggression in nonadjudicated samples (Hall, 1990; Thompson et al., 2011). Additional research is needed on the wide range of factors that could contribute to sexual assault and, more specifically, on the characteristics of sexual assault perpetrators in the Air Force.

This report considers information on measures that have been or could be used for screening recruits who may be at risk for perpetrating sexual assault in the Air Force. The Air Force asked RAND to focus on the enlisted-accession process because 80 percent of the active-duty Air Force consists of enlisted personnel (Air Force Personnel Center [AFPC], 2015; Office of the Deputy Assistant Secretary of Defense, 2013).[5] This research may have implications for officer accessions as well.

This report reviews the Air Force's current recruitment and preenlistment screening practices for those applying to become enlisted personnel and considers the extent to which these address sexual assault prevention. It also reviews previous research on integrity tests, or honesty tests, and screening methods, such as background assessments and personality-based tests, used in other contexts. Organizations frequently use such tests to screen out job applicants who may have an increased likelihood of counterproductive workplace behaviors, such as theft or other

---

[5] Similarly, approximately 80 percent or more of the Air National Guard and Air Force Reserves consisted of enlisted personnel (Office of the Deputy Assistant Secretary of Defense, 2013).

dishonest behaviors. The report describes different elements of and limitations to these measures and considers their potential applicability for preemployment screening for preventing sexual assault in the Air Force.

Approach

To address Air Force options for screening, we first conducted in-depth discussions with representatives from the U.S. Air Force Recruiting Service (AFRS) and individuals who facilitate the screening process at the San Antonio Military Entrance Processing Station (MEPS) in December 2013. During these meetings, individuals spoke with us regarding the general recruitment and accession process for enlisted airmen. Topics included key steps in the process, eligibility for becoming an enlisted airman, and screening tools currently in place. The meetings also addressed the waiver process in general and moral waivers specifically, as well as information that recruits receive on sexual assault and sexual-harassment policies in the Air Force. We requested materials that meeting attendees felt were relevant for understanding the Air Force recruitment and accession process. These materials included forms completed during the preenlistment screening process, PowerPoint files, instrument reports, and records of waivers. Section 2 describes much of the information we obtained from these materials.

We also reviewed previous research on integrity tests and other measures, including background assessments and personality-based assessments. In doing so, we considered (1) general information on integrity testing; (2) integrity tests in the armed forces; (3) measures of workplace aggression, maltreatment, and incivility; and (4) measures that may be associated with sexual harassment and sexual aggression. We searched English-language literature published since January 1990 using keywords and phrases relevant to each of these areas. After establishing a preliminary list of relevant studies, we reviewed the references listed in the studies to identify additional research. We also asked informed colleagues to review this list and identify research that might have been overlooked. Section 3 summarizes the information from this literature review.

Study Limitations

This report focuses on measures used in employment settings and includes some etiological work on sexual assault. It is beyond the scope of this report to thoroughly review theory and previous research on measures associated with sexual assault; these topics are discussed in another RAND report (Greathouse et al., 2015), which more thoroughly addresses methods and literature on predicting sexual assault perpetration.

The literature reviewed in this report indicates that no available employment-screening tools are strongly predictive of future sexual assault behaviors. Thus, no "off-the-shelf" measure for identifying applicants or employees who are highly prone to perpetrate sexual assault currently exists. Therefore, this report broadly reviews research on general personnel-screening measures and considers several measures that previous research has suggested may be associated with sexual assault proclivity.

Organization of the Report

Section 2 reviews Air Force recruiting policies and procedures, considering the extent to which they address proclivity toward sexual assault. It describes the Air Force's Intervene, Dissuade, Deter, Detect, and Accountability (ID3A) program and provides an overview of the policies and procedures in the initial recruitment process, including preliminary screening with the recruiter and MEPS personnel. It also considers the Air Force waiver process for recruits with potentially disqualifying characteristics. It then considers personnel-screening measures that other organizations, businesses, and the military use.

Section 3 provides information on integrity tests, research on and use of these tests in personnel selection, categories of integrity tests, and validity of these tests. It then considers the applicability of integrity tests for assault prevention.

Section 4 reviews how the Air Force may apply this material to its screening process and provides preliminary recommendations for the service's sexual assault prevention efforts.

2. Addressing Sexual Assault Prevention in Air Force Recruitment

AFRS reviews the criminal records of all enlisted applicants prior to admission and, unless a waiver is granted, screens out those who have been convicted of violent crimes, including sexual assault (Air Force Policy Directive 36-60; Air Force Instruction 36-6001). Recruitment and enlistment policies and procedures that address sexual assault may serve as the Air Force's first line of defense against this crime within the service. This section reviews existing policies and procedures, focusing on how they address risks of sexual assault perpetration.

Air Force Recruiting Policies and Procedures

As part of its recruitment goals, the Air Force sought to recruit 26,275 individuals to join its enlisted force in 2013. To achieve this goal, it employed 1,987 recruiters at 1,901 facilities. In the recent past, the Air Force employed a monthly quota-and-incentive system to promote enlistments, allotting differing points and benefits to different categories of accessions and contracts (Oken and Asch, 1997). During summer 2015, the Air Force converted from a system based on incentives to one based on markets and mission objectives.

The Air Force's recruitment and enlistment process has several steps, and multiple individuals may interact with applicants at each step. However, the recruiter is often the individual with whom applicants interact most regularly and with whom applicants are most familiar during the recruitment process. An applicant's close relationship with a recruiter has the potential to turn unprofessional, which may taint perceptions of Air Force culture, values, and allowable behaviors (Davis, 2013). From 2007 to 2009, there were between 0.6 and 1.7 substantiated allegations of any form of recruiter misconduct per 100 Air Force recruiters per fiscal year (FY; Asch and Heaton, 2010). Two percent of these allegations involved sexual misconduct, and 48 percent involved fraternization.[6] The Air Force has instituted several new policies in its efforts to prevent sexual misconduct of recruiters, although the efficacy of these policies has not been clearly established.

Recruiters must be highly familiar with the Air Force procedures for identifying and qualifying the thousands of recruit candidates for enlistment.[7] Recruiters thus tend to have several years of experience in the service. Most Air Force recruiters are staff sergeants (E-5) and, on average, have 10 to 12 years of service experience (Haygood, 2013). The Air Force carefully defines and closely monitors appropriate Air Force recruiter behavior toward applicants, as

---

[6] False promise or coercion constituted an additional 2 percent of allegations, and concealment or falsification constituted the remaining 48 percent.

[7] Different procedures exist for enlistment and commissioning. Because most who join the Air Force do so through enlistment, this report focuses on enlistment procedures.

discussed below. Recruiters are strictly prohibited from unprofessional relationships with applicants.

Intervene, Dissuade, Deter, Detect, and Accountability

The Air Force's ID3A program seeks to hold airmen accountable for their actions toward others. ID3A involves eliminating, or dissuading, airmen's inclinations to misbehave by selecting individuals with a demonstrated history of appropriate behavior, through psychological screening, and through training that emphasizes the importance of professional behavior. Although professional behavior in the Air Force may be defined in many ways, it includes zero tolerance for sexual discrimination, harassment, and assault (HQ AFRS, 2013). Sanctions— including counseling, reprimand, removal, demotion, adverse comments on performance reports, separation, and even courts martial—are in place to deter unprofessional behaviors among airmen. Leader involvement, video surveillance, feedback mechanisms, and awareness are among the tools that the Air Force uses to promote detection and accountability (Welsh, 2013). Although the Air Force has several general policies associated with ID3A, it has not enumerated specific actions and policies that are part of it and has not established whether the program has reduced incidents of sexual assault. Generally, educating individuals on such behaviors as sexual assault may help prevent them (Anderson and Whitson, 2005; Rothman and Silverman, 2007).[8] This report focuses on recruitment and screening in the Air Force. However, the Air Force should consider enumerating and evaluating the specific information and actions associated with the ID3A program or future iterations of this program.

The Air Force has applied the ID3A program to recruiter-applicant behaviors and relationships (Headquarters AFRS, 2013). Recruiters are responsible for communicating the guidelines for appropriate recruiter-applicant interactions to applicants prior to initial processing at a MEPS. This is outlined in the AFRS Commander Professional Relationship video, ID3A Rights/Responsibilities card, and ID3A Video Slide and Talking Points, which all applicants receive (HQ AFRS, 2013). These materials present applicants with the Air Force core values— integrity first, service before self, and excellence in all that airmen do. They also inform applicants of the appropriate way to think of and behave toward their recruiters.

Recruiters are responsible for abiding by and requiring applicants to abide by a professional relationship contract and the Air Force Policy on Recruiter Assistance Program airmen relationships (HQ AFRS, 2013). These materials specify that the recruiter and applicant will not attempt or establish an intimate or sexual relationship, applicants should not feel pressured to engage in unprofessional behavior with the recruiter, and applicants must report any unprofessional behavior involving the recruiter. Recruiters must review and require applicants to sign the Air Force Rights and Duties of an U.S. Air Force trainee form (HQ AFRS, 2013), and

---

[8] Prevention is broader than education and attitude change. For example, it may also include other behavioral interventions, such as for alcohol consumption (Abbey, McAuslan, and Ross, 1998; Farris and Hepner, 2014).

they must provide a book to each recruit that outlines fundamental aspects of becoming a professional airman.[9] These materials serve as part of the initial efforts of the Air Force to dissuade individuals misbehaving in these ways while in the service.

Policies and Procedures in the Initial Recruitment Process

Above and beyond outlining appropriate recruiter-applicant relationships and informing applicants of general behaviors that the Air Force considers professional and unprofessional, AFRS takes a series of actions during the recruitment process to disqualify individuals with certain characteristics. Many of the potentially disqualifying characteristics for Air Force applicants involve distinct mental-health concerns and records of problem behaviors, including aggravated assault with a deadly weapon, rape, and sexual harassment (AFRS Instruction 36-2001, 2012). Such policies may prevent those with a higher likelihood of committing sexual assault from joining the Air Force, although there has been no analysis of their efficacy for preventing sexual assault in the service. Such analysis of policy efficacy may be difficult because, as noted later in this section, much of this information is not recorded electronically. AFRS may consider recording and maintaining applicant data in a database.

Preliminary Screening Prior to Formal Appointment

After an individual, or "lead," expresses interest in an Air Force career, a recruiter will typically review several prequalification criteria with that lead before scheduling a formal appointment (Air Education and Training Command [AETC], 2008). Figure 2.1 illustrates the initial process. Air Force policy does not require the recruiter to review qualification criteria at the preappointment stage. No checklist or form must be completed at the preliminary screening. Rather, as AFRS personnel indicated during discussions for this research, this preliminary assessment is considered to be typical and useful but not obligatory.

During the typical preliminary assessment, the recruiter may conduct an informal review that covers several broad areas, including citizenship, conscientious objector status, morals, age, prior service, physical, education, drugs, dependents, and Social Security number (CCMAPPEDDS; U.S. Air Force, 2014). In reviewing these criteria, the recruiter will ask applicants whether they are citizens or legal residents of the United States, whether they are conscientious objectors or have personal beliefs that would stop them from conducting certain duties, and whether they have a documented history of antisocial behavior that would disqualify them from consideration. Further, the recruiter will also assess whether the applicant falls within the appropriate age range (i.e., between 17 and 39 years of age for non–prior service [NPS] applicants who will go to basic

---

[9] The Professional Development Guide (Air Force Pamphlet 36-2241, 2013), is provided to recruits entering into the DEP.

Figure 2.1. Initial Processing of Applicant for Air Force Enlistment

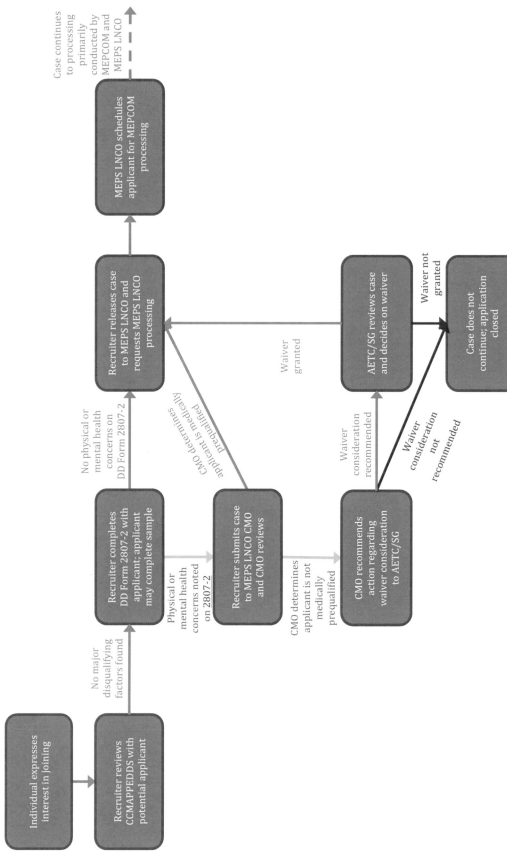

NOTE: Green lines and arrows indicate applicant advancement through the application process to Air Force entry. Yellow arrows and lines indicate delays in advancement through the process, and red arrows and lines indicate that the application process is discontinued.

military training [BMT]); whether the applicant has prior experience in the Air Force or a military service; whether the applicant meets certain height, weight, and physical ability requirements; and what level of education the applicant has completed. The recruiter will request information regarding the applicant's substance use or abuse, custody of dependents, and Social Security number. Should an informal review of these criteria indicate that the applicant appears to be eligible, the recruiter will schedule a formal appointment.

Of the above criteria, those that may be most relevant to reducing the likelihood that sexual assault perpetrators will join the Air Force are those regarding antisocial behaviors and history of substance abuse. Individuals may volunteer information or respond to recruiter questions about prior history of perpetration of rape, indecent assault, or sexual harassment, or they may volunteer information or respond to recruiter questions about their history of alcohol or drug abuse. Eliminating individuals with a history of sexual assault perpetration and substance abuse may reduce the number of individuals likely to perpetrate sexual assault in the future, as research has repeatedly shown these to be significant risk factors (Loh et al., 2005). Whether an individual is explicitly asked about a history of behavior related to sexual assault can vary, based on the topics a particular recruiter perceives to be of most importance. Standardized, explicit questions on these topics would allow a more-thorough initial review of applicants.

Prequalification and Prescreening with Formal Appointment

During a formal recruitment appointment, the applicant may be asked to complete a sample Armed Services Vocational Aptitude Battery (ASVAB), which assesses arithmetic reasoning, word knowledge, paragraph comprehension, and mathematics knowledge. The recruiter will also obtain information about the applicant that will permit formal determination of eligibility for the Air Force and complete Directives Division (DD) Form 2807-2, Accessions Medical Prescreen Report, for the applicant. DD Form 2807-2 addresses several physical conditions, such as arthritis, epilepsy, or heart murmurs, that may disqualify an individual from joining the Air Force or that may disqualify an individual from entering certain career fields after joining. This form also addresses mental-health conditions that may disqualify an applicant. These conditions include (1) a history of having seen a psychiatrist, psychologist, social worker, counselor, or other mental-health professional; (2) previous rejection from military service; (3) discharge from military service for medical reasons; (4) participation in drug or alcohol rehabilitation; (5) evaluation, treatment, or hospitalization for alcohol abuse, dependence, or addiction; and (6) evaluation, treatment, or hospitalization for substance use, abuse, addiction, or dependence.

DD Form 2807-2 addresses characteristics that may be associated with sexual assault, including substance abuse. However, it does not explicitly ask individuals whether they have ever been charged with or accused of sexual assault or sexual harassment. At this stage, either the applicant would have to volunteer such information, or the recruiter would need to obtain it some other way. One Air Force recruiter noted that this is the stage at which applicants are asked to self-report moral qualifying information (see Appendix A and next section for examples).

Questions on sexual assault or sexual harassment could be asked at this stage or, as noted later, at other stages in the screening process.

Potentially disqualifying answers on DD Form 2807-2 do not automatically result in permanent disqualification from consideration for the service. Rather, additional documentation must be obtained before an individual can be fully considered for the Air Force or for certain career fields in the Air Force. If an applicant's answers suggest that their moral suitability for the Air Force is in question, a moral eligibility determination will be completed. The information in the additional documentation requested can help determine eligibility. Prior to scheduling an applicant for physical processing, the recruiter will send a copy of the DD Form 2807-2 to the MEPS Medical Section for review. For mental-health issues, documentation regarding past or present counseling or treatment must be obtained and sent to the MEPS Chief Medical Officer (CMO). Using the information provided in DD Form 2807-2 and additional documentation submitted, the CMO will determine whether an applicant with potentially disqualifying answers on DD Form 2807-2 is in fact qualified to apply to join the Air Force.

If the applicant either has not indicated yes to any of the elements in DD Form 2807-2 or has indicated yes to elements but the CMO has determined the applicant is qualified, the applicant's case file will be released to the MEPS liaison noncommissioned officer (LNCO). The recruiter will also ask the MEPS LNCO to schedule an applicant for additional processing, and the MEPS LNCO will schedule a time for applicant processing at Military Entry Processing Command (USMEPCOM). If the CMO determines that the applicant is not medically prequalified, the recruiter and the recruiter's supervisor may request a waiver for the applicant from the AETC Surgeon General (SG). Applicants receiving the waiver proceed with MEPS processing; the application process ends for those who do not receive a waver.

Air Force Waiver Process

As noted, an individual with potentially disqualifying answers on DD Form 2807-2 may seek a waiver for further consideration. The need for a waiver may be noted during the prequalification and prescreening process or later in the application process. This may include, for example, when the applicant completes Standard Form (SF) 86, Questionnaire for National Security Positions, which the military services and others use as part of the application for a security clearance and includes items regarding psychological health and police records. Generally, recruiters may pursue waivers for particularly promising applicants. Depending on the case characteristics, different levels of authority are required to grant a waiver (AFRS Instruction 36-3001, 2012).

A recruiter may request a waiver for an applicant for a variety of reasons, including physical conditions. Moral offenses and waivers for them may be of most relevance to deterring current and potential future sexual assault perpetrators from joining the Air Force. A moral-eligibility determination must be completed when an applicant admits to or was charged with, but not adversely adjudicated for, offenses requiring a waiver (AFRS Instruction 36-3001, 2012). Five categories of moral offenses require waivers in the Air Force. Each category varies in level of severity of offenses, with category 1 being the most severe and category 5 being the least severe. Category 1 and 2 offenses require waiver approval from a higher level of command than do category 3, 4, and 5 offenses.[10]

Category 1 moral offenses involve major misconduct, such as rape, aggravated assault with a deadly weapon, manslaughter, and murder.[11] Appendix A provides example offenses (AFRS Instruction 36-3001, 2012). Individuals convicted of or adversely adjudicated on one or more of these offenses can enter the Air Force only with a waiver from the AFRC commander or vice commander, which means only an Air Force general officer or colonel can make this decision. AFRS personnel noted that waivers for these offenses are extremely rare and that, usually, the individual is permanently disqualified from service. Completely eliminating waivers for these offenses is a potential course of action for the Air Force, but this option is not currently under consideration. Since these waivers are already extremely rare, such action may have minimal impact on reducing sexual assault in the Air Force.

Category 2 moral offenses involve sexual harassment, indecent assault, and offenses for which maximum confinement under local law exceeds one year. Like Category 1 offenses, conviction of or adverse adjudication on one of these offenses is considered to be disqualifying for Air Force entry and requires applicants to receive a waiver from a recruiting group commander or deputy commander. A "group" is one organizational level below the AFRS headquarters and is led by an Air Force colonel.

A moral offense is considered to fall into category 3 if the maximum possible confinement under local law exceeds four months but is less than one year. Individuals convicted or adversely adjudicated on a category 3 offense are disqualified from joining the Air Force and require a waiver from a recruiting squadron commander before their application will be considered further. A recruiting squadron is one organizational level below a group and is led by a lieutenant colonel. Category 3 moral offenses include indecent exposure, public drunkenness, and drunk and disorderly behavior.

An offense falls into category 4 if the maximum confinement under local law is four months or less. An individual may be disqualified from joining the Air Force if convicted or adversely adjudicated on two category 4 offenses within the last three years or if convicted or adversely adjudicated on three or more category 4 offenses in a lifetime. Like category 3 offenses, waiver

---

[10] For alternative moral waiver system, see, for example, Army Regulation 601-210.

[11] For Air Force moral eligibility determination, Air Force Recruiting Service Instruction 36-2001 (2012, p. 39) defines rape as

> [a]ny intentional sexual contact, characterized by use of force, threats, intimidation, abuse of authority, or when the victim does not or cannot consent, including when due to incapacitation by drugs or alcohol. In addition, any offenses classified, as "rape (including statutory rape)," "forcible sodomy," and "other unwanted sexual contact that is aggravated, abusive, or wrongful" or attempts to commit one of these offenses.

approval rises to the level of the recruiting squadron commander. Example category 4 moral offenses include fighting or participating in a brawl and purchase, possession, or consumption of alcoholic beverages by a minor.

Finally, most category 5 moral offenses involve misbehavior related to driving (e.g., driving on shoulder). Individuals who, in any 365-day period over the past three years, have been convicted or adversely adjudicated on at least six such offenses, or on five category 5 offenses and one traffic-related category 4 offense, are considered ineligible for Air Force entry. The recruiting squadron commander is responsible for making decisions on waiver applications for such offenses. AFRS collects some information on the number of different waivers by type, although not by category of offense. Table 2.1 shows data from AFRS on waivers by type from 2008–2011 (Haygood, undated). These waiver types correspond with those the Office of the Secretary of Defense (OSD) has outlined for tracking and reporting (Department of Defense Instruction 1304.32, 2013). Since 2008, the proportion of NPS accessions with waivers ranged from 2 to 9 percent. The most prevalent type of waiver granted varies by year, with a large number of conduct-based waivers granted in 2008, and a large number of medical waivers granted in 2011.

Across all waivers, preliminary research suggests that those with waivers have a 2.6 percent higher attrition rate than those without waivers. The rates of four-year attrition across individuals who have received the different types of waivers (conduct, finance, drug, or other) are about equal (AFPC, 2010). Differences do appear when examining the number of unfavorable information files (UIFs) for individuals who have received the different types of waivers.[12] Specifically, those with waivers for conduct or drugs tend to have a higher proportion of UIFs on their military records, suggesting there are more concerns associated with their performance and behavior.

Prequalification and Prescreening Conducted Primarily at USMEPCOM and MEPS LNCO

Figure 2.2 picks up the application process with applicants' arrival at USMEPCOM for their processing appointments. Here, applicants may be given the full ASVAB, but AFRS personnel commented that an applicant may have completed the ASVAB earlier, such as during a high school testing session or at one of 65 military entrance testing sites.

Applicants are also given the Tailored Adaptive Personality Assessment System (TAPAS). This assessment was given to a subset of applicants for Air Force enlistment from 2009 to 2013 but has been administered to all Air Force applicants since July 2013. TAPAS takes 30 minutes or less to complete. TAPAS assesses personality traits, specifically facets of the "Big Five,"

---

[12] In defining UIFs, Air Force Instruction 36-2907 (2014, p. 4) notes that "the UIF is an official record of unfavorable information about an individual. It documents administrative, judicial, or non-judicial censures concerning the member's performance, responsibility and behavior."

Table 2.1. Number of Waivers by Type

	Fiscal Year						
	2008	**2009**	**2010**	**2011**	**2012**	**2013**	**2014**
Total NPS Air Force Active-Duty Enlisted NPS Accessions	27,765	31,780	28,363	28,265	28,757	26,022	24,020
Number with a waiver[a]	2,474	898	624	2,413	1,941	2,192	2,430
Percentage with a waiver	8.91	2.83	2.2	8.5	6.7	8.4	10.1
Total waivers by type[b]							
Aptitude	16	0	0	0	1,883	2,142	2,398
Medical	203	177	191	2,234	5	8	5
Conduct	1,839	375	131	48	57	61	49
Drug[c]	88	0[c]	0[c]	0	0	0	0
Other[d]	478	398	237	143			
Total	2,624	950	559	2,425	1,945	2,211	2,452
Law-violation conduct waivers (FY 2008)[e]							
Adult felony arrest(s) with convictions	0						
Juvenile felony arrest(s) with convictions	0						
Adult felony arrest(s) with no convictions	13						
Juvenile felony arrest(s) with no convictions	82						
Adjudicated misdemeanor offense(s)	1,104						
Adjudicated nontraffic offense(s)	496						
Adjudicated traffic offense(s)	144						
Law-violation conduct waivers (FYs 2009–2011)[f]							
Major misconduct arrest(s) and/or convictions		46	8	7	13	8	2
Major misconduct arrest(s) and/or no convictions		22	9	14	8	13	6
Misconduct offense(s) and/or convictions		181	20	19	19	20	29
Misconduct offense(s) and/or no conviction		53	7	7	13	17	9
One misconduct and four other nontraffic offense(s)		31	6	1	2	1	1
Five or more nontraffic offense(s)		35	1	0	2	12	2

SOURCE: Air Force Recruiting Information Support System. Data compiled by AFRS Production Emphasis and Competition Management Section from October 1, 2006 through September 30, 2013.
[a] This includes waiver of all types at all levels. A person with more than one waiver will only count once.
[b] Count each waiver approved separately—a person with a conduct waiver and medical waiver would have data entered in each.
[c] OSD counts only individuals who fail the drug test. U.S. Air Force policy does not currently allow such a waiver.
[d] For FYs 2007 and 2008, this count includes age, dependency, and other waivers. Only dependency waivers are counted for FYs 2009 and 2010.
[e] Reporting standards for FY 2008.
[f] Reporting standards changed in FY 2009 in order for all services to line up under a common O standard.

the five-factor model of personality (John and Srivastava, 1999): openness to experience, conscientiousness, extraversion, agreeableness, and neuroticism or emotional stability. The traits TAPAS assesses may influence an individual's ability to perform well in certain Air Force specialties, particularly as a battlefield airman (Stark et al., 2014).

Figure 2.2. Continued Processing of Applicant for Air Force Enlistment

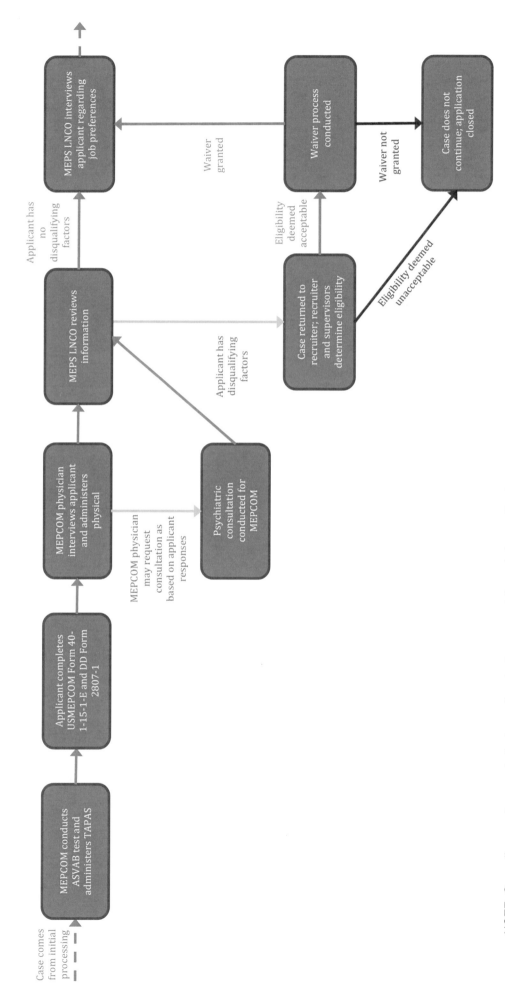

NOTE: Green lines and arrows indicate applicant advancement through the application process to Air Force entry. Yellow arrows and lines indicate a delay in advancement through the process, and red arrows and lines indicate that the application process is discontinued.

14

Currently, TAPAS is only used for selection for battlefield airman and related Air Force specialties. To reduce the likelihood that an applicant may provide misleading, socially desirable responses, each TAPAS item consists of two statements that are balanced in social desirability. The assessment asks applicants to choose the statement most descriptive of them. Items are administered using computer adaptive testing (also referred to as tailored testing). The test might present an item indicating a moderate level of a trait. A respondent who agrees with this item is then presented with a more "extreme" item assessing the same trait. A respondent disagreeing with the extreme item would then be presented with a less-extreme item. This approach is intended to estimate abilities or traits more precisely and be shorter than paper-and-pencil alternatives. As discussed in Section 3, TAPAS may be able to assist with screening for sexual assault perpetration among all applicants.

In addition to TAPAS, the applicant will be given forms to complete, and USMEPCOM medical personnel will conduct a physical examination (AETC, 2008). Before seeing medical personnel, the applicant will complete USMEPCOM Form 40-1-15-1-E, Medical History Provider Interview.[13] This form focuses on an applicant's history of mental and behavioral concerns, including depression, deliberate self-injury, suicide attempts, arrests, school suspensions, firings, removal from home, traffic violations, difficulty sleeping, and alcohol consumption. This form does not directly address violent behavior or history of sexual assault but would capture arrests for any of these behaviors.

In addition to completing USMEPCOM Form 40-1-15-1-E, the applicant will also be asked to complete DD Form 2807-1, Report of Medical History, which complements DD Form 2807-2. DD Form 2807-1 addresses whether an applicant currently has or has ever had various physical concerns, readdressing those listed on DD Form 2807-2. This form also addresses mental-health concerns that may disqualify an applicant. Many of these are different from those on DD Form 2807-2. Specifically, an applicant must complete information regarding the following: (1) nervous troubles, including anxiety and panic attacks; (2) habitual stammering, (3) amnesia or neurological symptoms; (4) difficulty sleeping; (5) receipt of counseling; (6) depression or excessive worry; (7) evaluation and/or treatment for a medical condition, (8) suicide attempts; and (9) use of illegal drugs. Applicants are also asked whether they have previously been rejected for or discharged from military service. Applicants answering yes to any of the questions on this form must provide information on dates, names of doctors, and treatment. USMEPCOM medical personnel use this as part of their assessment of applicants. However, this information is never entered into a database, which hinders assessment of form validity. DD Form 2807-1 does not include questions on history of sexual assault; including such questions could make this background assessment more thorough.

After completing these forms, the applicant will see a USMEPCOM physician. That physician will review the forms the applicant has just completed, interview the applicant about

---

[13] There is no threat of legal repercussions if an applicant does not disclose on this form.

the responses, and conduct a physical assessment. During the interview and assessment, the physician will complete DD Form 2808, Report of Medical Examination. This form addresses multiple physical conditions of the applicant, including blood pressure, dental defects, and vision. The physician will also address neurologic and psychiatric symptoms. The primary role of the USMEPCOM physician is to perform a physical assessment, but applicant responses during the interview may lead the physician to perceive elements associated with suicide risk or impulsivity. One USMEPCOM physician noted that, if concerns about the psychological health of an applicant arise during this interview, the USMEPCOM physician may request a psychiatric consult.

Once the USMEPCOM physician has completed the physical and, if needed, a psychiatric consult, the applicant's files are submitted to the MEPS LNCO, who will review the files for any potential disqualifications. If there are no disqualifying factors, the MEPS LNCO will interview the applicant regarding job preferences. If there are potential disqualifying factors, the applicant's case is returned to the recruiter. The recruiter and the recruiter's supervisors will then review the files to determine whether the recruit's application may continue. The recruiter and supervisors may pursue a waiver to continue the application. If the waiver is granted, the case continues with the MEPS LNCO. If the waiver is not pursued or granted, the application is closed. As noted previously, waivers are rarely pursued for certain categories of moral offenses, including categories 1 and 2.

Continued Qualification and Screening of Applicant

After an applicant has been interviewed about job preferences, the process continues as depicted in Figure 2.3. The MEPS LNCO will initiate the security-investigation process (AETC, 2008). This investigation process requires the applicant to complete SF-86, Questionnaire for National Security Positions. This form requires detailed information about applicants' history for the past seven to ten years. The form addresses such areas as police records, mental and emotional health, illegal use of drugs or drug activity, and personal references. After completion of the form, a thorough investigation into additional details of an applicant's history will be conducted. This investigation typically requires several months to complete and may not be completed until after an individual has completed BMT, depending on the length of time the recruit must wait before attending BMT. If the investigation returns information that may prevent an individual from receiving a security clearance, that case is returned to the recruiter, and the recruiter and supervisors determine eligibility. The investigation process may elicit or reveal disqualifying factors. AFRS personnel noted that the process would likely reveal a history of morally disqualifying behavior. For example, the process may uncover information about a history of rape or sexual assault, particularly if there are police records. If disqualifying factors are identified, the applicant's file will be returned to the recruiter. In coordination with superiors, the recruiter will either pursue the waiver process or close the application. If the recruiter pursues the waiver process and if a waiver is granted, the case will continue.

16

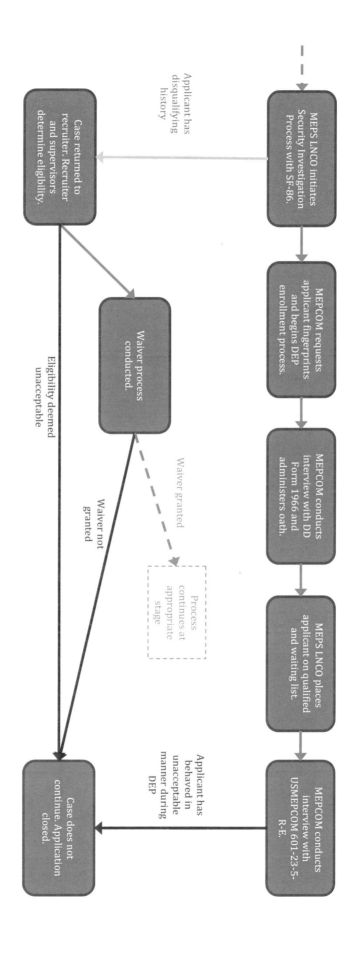

Figure 2.3. Final Processing of Applicant for Air Force Enlistment

MEPS LNCO initiates Security Investigation Process with SF-86.

MEPCOM requests applicant fingerprints and begins DEP enrollment process.

MEPCOM conducts interview with DD Form 1966 and administers oath.

MEPS LNCO places applicant on qualified and waiting list.

MEPCOM conducts interview with USMEPCOM 601-23-5-R-E.

Applicant has disqualifying history

Case returned to recruiter. Recruiter and supervisors determine eligibility.

Waiver process conducted.

Waiver granted

Process continues at appropriate stage

Waiver not granted

Eligibility deemed unacceptable

Applicant has behaved in unacceptable manner during DEP

Case does not continue. Application closed.

NOTE: Green lines and arrows indicate applicant advancement through the application process to Air Force entry. Yellow arrows and lines indicate a delay in advancement through the process, and red arrows and lines indicate that the application process is discontinued.

Once SF-86 has been completed with MEPS LNCO, USMEPCOM will obtain the applicant's fingerprints and begin the Delayed Entry Program (DEP) enrollment process. But before the individual enters the DEP, USMEPCOM will conduct a preenlistment interview with DD Form 1966, Record of Military Processing. During this interview, information about the applicant's education, marital status, birthplace, birthdate, and previous military service history will be reviewed. In addition, applicants are be asked about their criminal history, specifically whether they have ever had problems with a law-enforcement agency, have ever been arrested, have ever been to court, have court cases pending, have traffic tickets or fines, have fines for drug or alcohol incidents, are currently on parole or probation, or have been told to enlist by a law enforcement agency. They will also be asked about their drug use. USMEPCOM personnel do not ask questions about incidents of sexual assault. After this interview, USMEPCOM will administer the Oath of Enlistment, as required by federal statute in 10 U.S. Code 502. USMEPCOM will then place the individual on a waiting list, and the individual will participate in DEP while waiting to begin BMT. There is a variable wait time before a recruit is sent to BMT, and a recruit may have to wait several weeks or months before attending BMT. For those who have to wait several months, DEP involves, at a minimum, monthly meetings with the recruiter and may also involve physical training.

A BMT ship date will be assigned. On that ship date, USMEPCOM will conduct a preaccession interview, using USMEPCOM Form 601-23-5-R-E, Introductory Preaccession Interview. At this time, an individual is informed that they must provide any new or changed information that has arisen during DEP. In addition, questions regarding drug use will be asked. Specifically, the interviewer will ask the applicant whether they have used or sold marijuana during DEP. They will also be asked whether they have had trouble of any kind due to marijuana or alcohol use and whether they have had psychiatric care or counseling or have attempted to commit suicide. If the applicant has no new issues, the applicant will proceed to enlistment. If the recruit identifies issues at this stage, the recruit is returned to the LNCO, and a determination will be made about whether the recruit will ship to BMT or not.

Postscreening of Applicant

Although not part of the initial Air Force recruitment and screening, it is worth noting that the Air Force administers an additional assessment during BMT that addresses trainees' behavioral and mental health issue. Specifically, within the first three days of BMT, trainees receive the Lackland Behavioral Questionnaire (Garb, Wirick, and Wood, 2012). This questionnaire addresses the following topics, among others: anger, depression, history with police, history with psychiatric medication, suicidal tendencies, behavioral problems in high school, substance abuse, history of psychotherapy, and history of theft or destruction of property. The primary purpose of this assessment is not to screen trainees out from the service. Rather, the Air Force uses trainees' responses to this questionnaire to identify individuals who may be at risk for future problematic behaviors and to determine whether and what recommendations and referrals the individuals may need (e.g., mental health counseling, substance-abuse counseling). Research has demonstrated that this questionnaire significantly predicts separation due to mental health or behavioral issues (Garb et al., 2013). By including items in the questionnaire that address the performance of or desire to perform behaviors that are sexually aggressive, the Air Force will be able to refer trainees to relevant counseling.

Conclusions and Recommendations

This section reviewed existing Air Force recruiting policies and procedures and considered their application to sexual assault prevention. Programs, materials, and presentations that contain accurate information about a job and organization, including both positive and negative aspects of these, serve as cues to applicants regarding what the organizational attributes are, and these cues may dissuade individuals who do not appreciate organizational norms from joining (Carless, 2005; Chapman et al., 2005; Earnest, Allen, and Landis, 2011). In addition, providing information that educates individuals on sexual assault may assist with its prevention (Anderson and Whitson, 2005; Rothman and Silverman, 2007). Thus, providing information about sexual assault and the Air Force's lack of tolerance for inappropriate relationships and sexual assault may serve as cues to applicants about Air Force norms and culture. This information may educate applicants and encourage those who do not appreciate these norms to self-select out of the process.

One program the Air Force currently has in place, ID3A, seeks to deter unprofessional behavior, which includes notifying recruiters and applicants of appropriate and inappropriate behaviors. This program provides little information about intolerance for sexual assault across the service (i.e., beyond recruiters and applicants) because BMT is considered the appropriate place to train incoming enlisted personnel on the seriousness of such acts. Although this program may deter sexual assault, the different elements of ID3A and the extent to which it has affected incidents of sexual assault in the Air Force have not been established. The Air Force may consider enumerating and evaluating the specific actions associated with ID3A, which would permit assessment of its impact, and expanding this program to include information beyond recruiter-applicant interactions.

Many potential disqualifications for Air Force applicants involve distinct mental-health concerns and records of problem behaviors. To the extent that these mental-health and behavioral concerns are associated with aggressive behaviors, using these disqualifiers may help screen out potential sexual assault perpetrators. For example, during prequalification and prescreening at a formal appointment with a recruiter, individuals must complete DD Form 2807-2, which addresses a history of elements that may be somewhat associated with sexual assault perpetration. However, this form does not explicitly ask applicants whether they have ever been charged with, accused of, or conducted a sexual assault. Applicants would therefore have to volunteer, or recruiters would have to make extra efforts to obtain, the information most relevant to possible future perpetration of sexual assault.

Applicants whose cases continue through the process will complete the TAPAS. This assessment contains several dimensions that may be associated with sexual assault proclivity, and the association of the measure's dimension with sexual assault proclivity could be considered to address its potential use in screening. In addition, applicants must complete USMEPCOM Form 40-1-15-1-E and DD Form 2807-1, both of which address past behaviors that may be associated with sexual assault perpetration. Neither form, however, asks specifically about an applicant's history of sexual assault or about sexual assault accusations made against the applicant. Again, more thorough inquiry into applicants' histories of sexual assault may assist in increased detection of those with such a history.

The Air Force currently has a moral eligibility determination requirement for applicants who admit to or are charged with, but not convicted of or adversely adjudicated for, offenses requiring a waiver, which include rape (AFRS Instruction 36-3001, 2012). During one of at least four points in the application process, the Air Force could ask applicants about their histories of sexual assault perpetration, which could include inquiring into whether or not there was a conviction. Potential points the Air Force could consider including this questioning are during initial review of CCMAPPEDDS with a potential applicant, during completion of DD Form 2807-2 with an applicant, during or after applicant completion of USMEPCOM Form 40-1-15-1-E and DD Form 2807-1, or during the preenlistment interview. More-thorough and standardized background assessments at these stages, specifically addressing previous sexually aggressive behavior, may help increase the likelihood that applicants will provide information on a history of sexual assault. If an applicant provides an affirmative response about prior sexually aggressive behavior, the Air Force may, at a minimum, require completion of a moral eligibility determination that must be reviewed by, at a minimum, a recruiting squadron commander. Therefore, including a question or set of questions on sexual assault perpetration could improve the Air Force's ability to detect these behaviors. In addition, electronic collection and recording of this information could help determine the validity of this and other forms for detecting applicants with a proclivity to perpetrate sexual assault.

Finally, an Air Force applicant must complete a security-investigation process, including SF-86. This form requires an applicant to provide detailed information regarding their history over the past seven to ten years, and the associated investigation may reveal information about a history of rape or sexual assault perpetration. The files of applicants with potential disqualifications are returned to their recruiters, who may, with their superiors, pursue waivers or close applications. Individuals who have been convicted of sexual assault are highly unlikely to receive a waiver.

3. Review and Consideration of the Applicability of Various Measures for Sexual Assault Prevention

This section reviews measures that organizations, businesses, and the military use or may use as part of employee screening and considers their applicability for addressing sexual assault perpetration. Such measures may be used to predict negative behaviors, including violence and aggression, among employees or applicants for employment. For example, integrity tests, also known as honesty tests, are used to predict job performance and counterproductive workplace behaviors—behaviors, such as theft or drug use, that violate employers' interests (Camara and Schneider, 1994; Guastello and Rieke, 1991). Integrity tests tend to be paper-and-pencil or computer-based instruments (but also see Hollwitz and Pawlowski, 1997 for information on interview-based methods) and may be administered during the applicant-screening process. Although various businesses and organizations frequently use these, some researchers have criticized using such tests for personnel selection, noting their potentially low validity and susceptibility to deception or faking (Morgeson et al., 2007). Additional measures, which are not considered to be integrity tests (e.g., personality assessment, background checks) may also be used to predict negative behaviors, including sexual aggression and proclivity for sexual assault. However, these assessments may have many of the same limitations as integrity tests, including low validity.[14] This section reviews the history of integrity testing and describes previous research addressing its strengths and limitations. The section then reviews additional measures that may be associated with negative or aggressive behaviors. Throughout, the discussion considers the application of these measures for sexual assault prevention efforts in the Air Force.[15]

Integrity Tests

The exact monetary and social costs of counterproductive workplace behaviors, including theft and antisocial behaviors, are not known. Past estimates suggest that employee theft costs American companies at least $200 billion each year (Appelbaum et al., 2006). In addition, almost two million American workers annually report being victims of nonfatal workplace violence

---

[14] Researchers have no single statistical standard to establish whether a measure is valid (see, for example, John and Soto, 2007). Some reports using correlations or corrected correlations for validity have suggested that coefficients of approximately 0.30 or above may be considered adequate (Saad et al., 1999). However, not only the size of the coefficient but also the nature of the criterion and sample characteristics should be considered (Roszkowski and Spreat, 2011).

[15] For additional information on characteristics and factors that may be associated with sexual assault perpetration, see Greathouse et al., 2015.

(Occupational Safety and Health Administration, 2002), and approximately 900 workplace homicides occur each year (Duhart, 2001). The consequences of hiring dishonest and violent employees have motivated businesses and organizations to detect and avoid employing individuals who may be particularly likely to exhibit inappropriate or antisocial workplace behaviors. To assist with identifying individuals who may be likely to exhibit such negative behaviors, businesses and organizations have incorporated various instruments into their employee screening processes.

Prior to 1988, polygraphs were not uncommon among U.S. businesses and organizations for detection of individuals likely to lie about their thoughts and past or present behaviors. Many integrity tests were developed for use where polygraphs were not permitted (Sackett, Burris, and Callahan, 1989). As more research questioned the use and effectiveness of polygraphs (e.g., Saxe, Dougherty, and Cross, 1985), Congress passed the Employee Polygraph Protection Act of 1988, prohibiting many U.S. employers from requiring or requesting that applicants or employees complete polygraphs but allowing exceptions for federal-, state-, and local-government employers. While the Air Force is permitted to use polygraphs, administering them to all Air Force accessions would be prohibitively costly.

Despite the general prohibition of polygraphs in 1988, employers remained interested in instruments that could identify applicants more likely to demonstrate counterproductive workplace behaviors. As a result, use and development of survey-style integrity tests continued. Multiple theories on the individual, situational, and cognitive underpinnings of counterproductive behaviors now exist, and many integrity tests based on these theories are available to employers (Martinko, Gundlach, and Douglas, 2002). Today, integrity testing is at least a $400-million-a-year industry (Stabile, 2002). Some of the more-popular integrity tests among employers are the London House Personnel Selection Inventory, the Reid Report, the Stanton Survey, the Personnel Reaction Blank, the Personnel Decisions International Employment Inventory Scales (Paajanen, Hansen, and McLellan, 1999), and the Reliability Scale of the Hogan Personality Series (Hogan and Hogan, 2007; Sackett and Wanek, 1996). These tests generally fall into two categories: overt and personality oriented.

Categories of Integrity Tests

Overt and personality-based integrity tests use questions designed to address somewhat different but overlapping content areas (Ones, Viswesvaran, and Schmidt, 1993 ; Sackett, Burris, and Callahan, 1989). The purposes of overt integrity tests, including direct assessment of attitudes toward counterproductive thoughts and actions, may be clear not only to potential employers but also to applicants. These tests may include questions that address rationalizations about and perceived ease of theft (Ryan and Sackett, 1987). Such a question might be phrased as a statement, e.g., "Cheating on an expense account isn't really stealing." The tests may also include assessments of the applicant's history of counterproductive behaviors (e.g., dollar value of all that an applicant has stolen from work). The London House Personnel Selection Inventory, the Reid Report, and the Stanton Survey are some of the more commonly used overt integrity tests. Because applicants can easily determine the purpose of these tests, employers express concern that applicants may provide misleading responses on or react negatively to these tests (Ryan and Sackett, 1987).

Personality-based assessments are considered to be more covert, or disguised-purpose, forms of integrity tests, such that it may not be clear to applicants or employees what job-relevant attributes the items address. These instruments build from measures of personality dimensions, such as the Big Five personality traits (e.g., conscientiousness, agreeableness, neuroticism [emotional stability]), to predict counterproductive behaviors (Ones, 1993). The use of personality-based assessments is based on research showing associations between personality traits and different workplace-relevant behaviors (Ones, Viswesvaran, and Schmidt, 1993). For example, research has shown that conscientiousness is negatively related to employee absence and positively related to job proficiency and training proficiency (Barrick and Mount, 1991; Judge, Martocchio, and Thoresen, 1997). Because personality-based assessments do not directly reference specific counterproductive behaviors, their purpose may be less obvious to applicants, which may mitigate some of the potential negative effects of overt integrity tests that concern employers. The Personnel Reaction Blank (Gough, 1972), the Personnel Decisions International Employment Inventory Scales (Paajanen, Hansen, and McLellan, 1999) and the Reliability Scale of the Hogan Personality Inventory (Hogan and Hogan, 2007) are all popular personality-based assessments (Sackett and Wanek, 1996).

Criterion-Related Validity for Integrity Tests

To support the use of integrity tests, research must demonstrate the tests' criterion-related validity. Criterion-related validity involves the extent to which a test is associated with indicators, or outcomes, of interest. One type of criterion-related validity *predictive validity*, in which test measurement occurring before the criterion behavior or construct of interest predicts that behavior or construct (National Research Council [NRC], 2003). Another type, *concurrent validity*, involves the extent to which a measure is associated with, rather than predictive of, indicators of interest. Integrity tests that show criterion-related validity must show an association between test scores and the counterproductive or productive workplace behaviors of interest (Ones and Viswesvaran, 2001).

Previous research has shown that both overt and personality-based integrity tests predict job performance, training performance, and counterproductive behaviors, including absenteeism and theft (e.g., Berry, Sackett, and Tobares, 2010; Berry, Sackett, and Wiemann, 2007; Cullen and Sackett, 2004; Ones, Viswesvaran, and Schmidt, 1993; Van Iddekinge et al., 2012). Integrity tests can also predict drug and alcohol abuse (Schmidt, Viswesvaran, and Ones, 1997). Different aspects of the tests, including whether they are overt or personality-based, may influence the extent to which the tests are associated with different behaviors. For example, overt and personality-based measures may be differentially associated with different behaviors.

Criteria for Overt and Personality-Based Tests

One of the most frequently cited assessments of the criterion-related validity of integrity tests is a meta-analysis of 665 validity coefficients (e.g., associations between tests scores and relevant ratings or behaviors), of which 389 are from overt integrity tests and 276 are from personality-based integrity tests (Ones, Viswesvaran, and Schmidt, 1993). This research considered two broad categories of criteria, job performance and general counterproductive behaviors. This meta-analysis showed that overt and personality-based tests were valid predictors of job performance and counterproductive behaviors (e.g., theft, illegal activities, tardiness, drug abuse, dismissals for theft). Overt tests had a validity of 0.33, and personality-based tests had a validity of 0.35, making them nearly equally valid in predicting job performance. Initial evidence suggested that the validity of overt integrity tests may be slightly higher, at 0.55, than that of personality-based tests, at 0.32, in predicting counterproductive behaviors.[16] However, Ones and her colleagues strongly discouraged others from placing great emphasis on the small difference between these two test types.

A later meta-analysis also considered the relationship between the two types of tests (Van Iddekinge et al., 2012). This research found that the validity of personality-based tests was slightly higher, at 0.18, than that of overt integrity tests, at 0.11, for addressing job performance. As with Ones, Viswesvaran, and Schmidt (1993), the validity of overt tests was higher, at 0.38, than that of personality-based assessments, at 0.27, for predicting counterproductive workplace behaviors. Differences across these meta-analyses in the observed average strength of validity coefficients may be due to differences in whether the assessment included studies conducted by those who do and do not publish (and sell) integrity tests or to differences how the meta-analyses considered the methodological rigor of included studies.

Although overt integrity tests may predict counterproductive behaviors better than personality-based assessments do, researchers generally suggest there is no clear evidence to support the use of one type of integrity test, overt or personality-based, over the other (see also Cullen and Sackett, 2004; Wanek, 1999). Additional research is needed to assess the predictive validity of new personality-based assessments. Measurement elements other than type of test may also influence the observed validity of integrity tests. For example, research has shown that the test publishers report "somewhat more optimistic" (Van Iddekinge et al., 2012, p. 511) criterion-related validities for job performance than nonpublishers do.[17] Integrity tests may also be differentially associated with measures obtained through different research methods. The breadth of measure (such as narrow measures that focus on one type of behavior, e.g., theft,

---

[16] As noted previously, some researchers have suggested that validity coefficients of 0.30 or above may be considered adequate (Saad et al., 1999).

[17] Notably, publishers and nonpublishers report roughly equal validities for counterproductive workplace behaviors (Van Iddekinge et al., 2012).

rather than broad measures that assess various counterproductive behaviors) and the sample used (such as applicant or employee) may also influence the observed validity of integrity tests.

Measurement Method

Counterproductive workplace behaviors can be measured in different ways. Self-reports of illegal behavior and supervisory ratings of counterproductive behaviors are two of the more common methods. Because of the common source of information (i.e., self), self-reports may be more strongly related to self-completed integrity tests than other ratings. Individuals possess more information on their own behaviors than do others, who may fail to detect an individual's illegal activities. Individuals may be able to bias their responses to integrity tests and self-reports in approximately the same manner. In early reviews of integrity tests, Sackett and his colleagues found high correlations between measures of integrity and self-admissions of counterproductive workplace behaviors (Sacket, Burris, and Callahan, 1989; Sackett and Harris, 1984). A subsequent meta-analysis showed stronger associations between integrity tests and self-admissions of behavior than between these tests and supervisory ratings (Ones, Viswesvaran, and Schmidt, 1993). More-recent research also showed stronger associations between self-reports of counterproductive behaviors and integrity tests than between these tests and either supervisory reports or employee records maintained by the company (Van Iddekinge et al., 2012).

Research has not yet addressed the cause of the stronger associations between integrity tests and self-reports. Thus, it is not clear whether the stronger association is due to similar levels of faking across assessments among employees or applicants. Perhaps because of the ambiguity of the results, many researchers discredit results from self-report (or self-admission) studies and exclude them when making substantive conclusions regarding integrity tests (e.g., Ones, Viswesvaran, and Schmidt, 1993). Additional research is needed to assess the associations between the different types of integrity tests (i.e., overt and personality-based) and different methods of criteria measurement.[18]

Breadth of Measure

Another potential moderator of the relationship between integrity test scores and behaviors is the breadth of measurement, which addresses whether a particular measure assesses a limited, specific set of behaviors, such as theft, or a broader category of generally disruptive behaviors. In general, instruments that measure at a breadth commensurate with the desired criterion are recommended (John and Benet-Martinez, 2000). Research on breadth of measure in the context of integrity testing has produced conflicting results. A meta-analysis found a slightly stronger association between integrity tests and theft criteria than between these tests and other disruptive

---

[18] If self-admissions are collected anonymously and if participants are confident that their responses cannot and will not be traced back to them, there may be less need to discredit results when making conclusions regarding integrity tests. However, an applicant's or an employee's anonymous responses cannot be used in their own employment screening process.

behaviors (e.g., violence on the job, tardiness, and absenteeism [Ones, Viswesvaran, and Schmidt, 1993]). However, subsequent research showed that these tests associated more strongly with broad measures of disruptive behaviors (e.g., tardiness, leaving work early, taking long or unauthorized work breaks, or being absent from work altogether) than with narrower measures of substance abuse, theft, or withdrawal (Van Iddekinge et al., 2012). Whether integrity tests are better predictors of broad or narrow criteria may depend on the breadth of both the integrity tests and the criteria used (Cullen and Sackett, 2004). For example, one may expect stronger associations between broad integrity tests and broad measures of counterproductive behaviors than between narrow integrity tests and broad measures of behaviors (Ones, 1993). Additional research is needed to assess these associations.

Type of Sample

In examining the criterion-related validity of integrity tests, researchers typically use two types of samples, either incumbent samples or applicant samples. Incumbents are current employees of an organization who have not previously been screened using an integrity test. Applicants are those applying for a particular position. Samples of applicants, particularly those employers wish to screen, are often the focal group for integrity tests. For both types of samples, the validities for integrity tests and both job performance and counterproductive workplace behaviors are fairly large. This suggests that integrity tests may be used with both samples, although research shows that validities for integrity tests and counterproductive workplace behaviors are higher for incumbent samples than for applicant samples (Ones, Viswesvaran, and Schmidt, 1993; Van Iddekinge et al., 2012). Researchers suggest that these results show applicants are more likely than current employees to provide misleading responses on integrity tests (Alliger and Dwight, 2000).

Construct Validity for Integrity Tests

In addition to assessing whether integrity tests are associated with, or predictive of, constructs of interest, research has also assessed the construct validity of these tests (Ones and Viswesvaran, 2001). As noted previously, criterion-related validity involves the extent to which the tests can be used predict measures of interest. Construct validity involves the extent to which integrity tests assess what they are intended to measure and thus addresses what concepts these tests tap into. Two methods for establishing construct validity are comparing the integrity test scores of different groups and examining the associations between other relevant measures and integrity test scores.

Contrasted Groups

Contrasting groups to validate integrity tests often involves examining the differences in integrity test scores between groups that are believed to differ in integrity or honesty (Ones, 1993). There have been relatively few contrasted-group assessments, but existing studies have compared incarcerated adults to job applicants (Sackett and Harris, 1984) and nurses who have had actions taken against their licenses compared to nurses from the general population (Kobbs and Arvey, 1993). If the tests are valid measures, those who are incarcerated or under investigation should show lower levels of integrity.

Indeed, previous research has shown significant and expected differences between contrasted groups. In one study, convicted felons scored lower than job applicants on the Reid Report, an overt integrity test (Ash, 1974). In another, nurses who had negative actions taken against their nursing licenses scored significantly lower than registered nurses from a broader population on the Personnel Reaction Blank, a personality-based integrity test (Kobbs and Arvey, 1993).

Associations Among Measures

Another method for assessing construct validity is to assess which measures integrity tests are associated with and the direction of these associations. Ones (1993) used primary and meta-analytic data to examine the associations between overt and personality-based integrity tests and the Big Five traits. She found that conscientiousness most strongly overlapped with these tests, and that agreeableness and neuroticism or emotional stability also strongly overlapped with both overt and personality-based integrity tests (also see Ones and Viswesvaran, 2001).

Additional research has considered the associations between integrity tests and other measures. Mumford et al. (2001) found that individual characteristics, including narcissism and power motives, were associated with scores on both overt and personality-based tests. Situational characteristics, such as alienation and negative peer-group exposure, were also associated with scores on the two test types and were more strongly related to test scores than were individual characteristics—leading to questions about whether integrity tests identify enduring individual characteristics, which is their intent, or more-malleable situational characteristics. A later review of the association between integrity tests and situational and individual characteristics concluded that both situational and individual characteristics influence scores, and researchers should perhaps consider the interaction between individual characteristics and social context to better understand scores (Berry, Sackett, and Wiemann, 2007).

Cognitive or mental-ability tests may also be used in employment screening. For example, as mentioned in Section 2, the Air Force uses scores on the ASVAB in applicant assessment. Cognitive ability tests are not considered to be integrity tests, but responses to these tests are associated with job performance and counterproductive work behaviors (Schmidt and Hunter, 1998; Dilchert et al., 2007). Some research also suggests sexual offenders have lower cognitive ability (Cantor et al., 2005). Researchers recommend using both integrity tests and tests of general mental ability for personnel selection (Ones and Viswesvaran, 2001; Schmidt and Hunter, 1998).

Possible Limitations of Integrity Tests

Although integrity tests are associated with job performance and counterproductive work behaviors, using integrity tests and other self-report measures to select employees has several potential problems (Camara and Schneider, 1994; Morgeson et al., 2007; Office of Technology Assessment [OTA], 1990). As noted earlier, respondent faking is a major concern for these tests. Other potential issues involve low base rates of the behaviors that they are designed to predict— a limited number of individuals will engage in certain counterproductive workplace behaviors (e.g., workplace theft, workplace violence)—and misclassification of individuals as unsuitable or suitable employees.

Faking Good

In integrity testing, *faking good* refers to respondents providing misleading responses to appear to be more-suitable employees. Overt integrity tests are highly susceptible to faking good (e.g., Guastello and Rieke, 1991), particularly among those with greater general cognitive ability (Brown and Cothern, 2002). For example, a job applicant could assume that an employer would prefer to hire applicants who disagree with the statement "Cheating on an expense account isn't really stealing." Thus, the applicant may report disagreement with the statement but actually feel agreement. Although designed to be less susceptible to faking good, personality-based tests also appear to be vulnerable (Morgeson et al., 2007).

Despite their susceptibility to faking good, integrity tests may remain valid predictors of job performance and counterproductive behaviors. For example, Ones et al. (2007, p. 1013) noted that "[t]he criterion-related validity of integrity tests is substantial, even in the potential presence of naturally occurring response distortion among job applicants." Ones et al. discounted laboratory experiments in which participants are either instructed to fake good or provide honest responses to integrity tests, noting that demand effects in the laboratory distort responses beyond what organizations may observe in real-world settings with real applicants (also see Hough and Oswald, 2000).

To address the potential effects of faking good, researchers have considered potential modifications to integrity tests. One such modification is use of forced-choice formats rather than the traditional single-stimulus (e.g., Likert scale) format. In the Likert format, participants are, for example, must indicate their level of disagreement or agreement with a sentence on a scale that ranges from 1 (strongly disagree) to 5 (strongly agree). Forced-choice formats require participants to select between items that appear to be similar in desirability for employment or similar in relevance for a particular job. Forced-choice formats may reduce, but not eliminate, the ability of job applicants to fake good (Jackson, Wroblewski, and Aston, 2000). Individuals with greater cognitive ability are better able to analyze and fake good on forced-choice inventories (Christiansen, Burns, and Montgomery, 2005), raising questions about whether cognitive ability confounds forced-choice integrity test results. To address this issue, researchers can control for cognitive ability when assessing forced-choice integrity tests (Vasilopoulos et al.,

2006). Other research suggests that forced-choice formats do not demonstrate sufficient resistance to faking in comparison to single-stimulus formats and thus are not a viable alternative for controlling faking (Heggestad et al., 2006). Still, researchers and theorists appear to perceive forced-choice formats to be promising for integrity testing (Morgeson et al., 2007). They also note that developing such tests requires a great deal of time, effort, and resources and that, if test security is compromised, additional tests must be developed.[19]

Additional methods used to address faking good include use of situational tests, which include conditional-reasoning tests. Conditional-reasoning tests present test takers with a scenario and ask them to select what they perceive to be a logical conclusion to this scenario within a provided set of response options. Participants are more likely to perceive certain response options as logical if they are using a particular justification mechanism. For example, those who are more aggressive may be more likely to perceive that the world is an aggressive place, which may bias their perceptions of how to respond to different scenarios (MacCann, Ziegler, and Roberts, 2011). Although promising, the validity of certain tests of conditional reasoning has been questioned (Berry, Sackett, and Tobares, 2010; Burroughs and James, 2005).

Cut Scores

Integrity tests often use cut scores, also known as cutoff scores or cutting scores, to establish whether an individual has "passed" the test. For example, individuals meeting or exceeding a particular cut score on an overt or personality-based integrity test will move forward through the employment selection process. If they do not meet the cut score, they may be eliminated from employment consideration.

Cut scores are established through various methods, and different methods used on the same test can lead to different cut scores (Berry and Sackett, 2009; Woehr, Arthur, and Fehrmann, 1991). For example, one set of methods for establishing a cut score involves first examining the relationship between test scores and the behavior or attitude of interest and then establishing a cut score based on that observed relationship (e.g., base rate). A second set of methods for establishing a cut score involves normative comparisons, such that cut scores are determined by the distribution of scores seen among available test takers (e.g., a certain number of standard deviations above or below the mean of test takers is used to establish the cut score).[20] A third set of methods involves establishing a standard for interpretive reference and then creating a cut score based on that standard. No single method is widely accepted for use in establishing cut scores on integrity tests (see Woehr, Arthur, and Fehrmann, 1991).

Reports disseminated by the American Psychological Association and OTA suggest that "There is overreliance on cut scores. Problems of labeling and false positive errors that have

---

[19] Computer adaptive testing can be used to protect test security.

[20] The Civil Rights Act of 1991 prohibits within-group norming on the basis of color, race, religion, sex, or national origin of assessments used for selection or referral of applicants for employment. For additional information, see Sackett and Wilk (1994).

dogged integrity tests are exacerbated by the use of cutting scores" (Camara and Schneider, 1994, p. 115). Specifically, test takers may be stigmatized, or labeled, based on where they score in relation to a cut score (Faust, 1996). Further, if integrity tests are reliable (e.g., a person receives the same or a similar score each time they take an integrity test) and if the tests suffer from false positive errors (see Dalton and Metzger, 1993), individuals will be systematically misclassified by cut scores and may be systematically denied employment. Options for addressing misclassification (e.g., institutional prediction) are described later in this section.

Low Base Rates

Other potential issues for integrity tests are using them to predict behaviors that occur relatively infrequently and their potential to misclassify respondents as unsuitable employees (OTA, 1990). Attempts to base employment decisions on measures designed to predict infrequent behaviors can lead to the exclusion of a large proportion of individuals who have not and would not conduct a behavior. Cut scores may be shifted to set a higher threshold for predicting infrequent behaviors, but this does not eliminate the issue of misclassification.

Misclassification

To illustrate the underlying issue of misclassification, one may consider possible test scores of two populations: one with and one without a given characteristic (see Figure 3.1). The distributions of test scores obtained from these two populations may be expected to overlap. This means that some individuals without the characteristic would have test scores that overlap with those of individuals with the characteristic, and some individuals with the characteristic would have test scores that overlap with the scores of individuals without the characteristic. To address incorrectly classifying someone as having or not having a characteristic, the test cut score can be shifted. For example, shifting the cut score to be more extreme may increase the likelihood of correctly classifying someone as having the characteristic (i.e., true positives) but may also increase the likelihood of incorrectly classifying someone as not having the characteristic (i.e., false negatives). By contrast, shifting the cut score to be less extreme may increase the likelihood of correctly classifying someone as not having the characteristic (i.e., true negatives) but may also increase the likelihood of incorrectly classifying someone as having the characteristic who does not (i.e., false positives). Many factors affect the likelihood of each of these correct and incorrect classifications, including the test criterion-related validity, behavior base rate, and cut score. For example, almost all classification errors made by a test of a characteristic with a lower base rate (i.e., seen in less of the population) will occur in misclassifying people as having the characteristic who do not (NRC, 2003; also see Appendix B).

Figure 3.1. Demonstration of the Classification of Two Populations Based on Responses to a Test

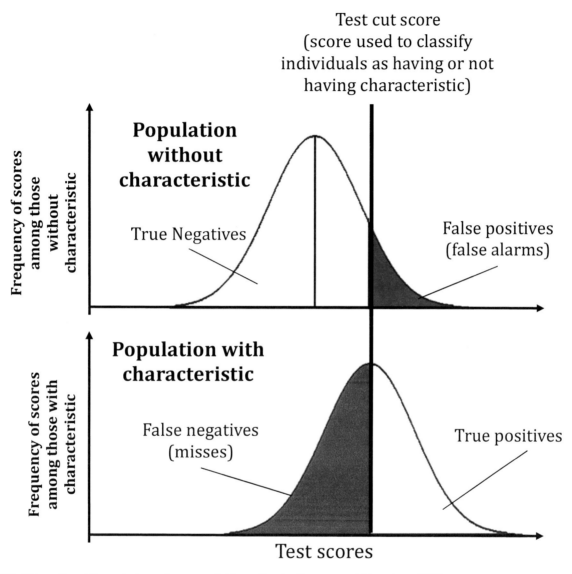

NOTE: This notional figure is based on a model from Swets, Dawes, and Monahan, 2000.

Researchers have considered the extent to which integrity tests may accurately or inaccurately categorize individuals, given the base rate for the behavior and accuracy of the test (NRC, 2003).[21] We provide examples of this assessment in Table 3.1 and in Appendix B. These examples illustrate that tests attempting to classify individuals based on their proclivity to conduct a relatively infrequent behavior are highly likely to misclassify individuals.

---

[21] Researchers have used different analyses for these assessments, including calculation of receiver operating characteristic curves (NRC, 2003) and direct application of Bayes' theorem (Martin, 1989). Similar assessments could be conducted using Air Force measures.

Table 3.1 shows the number of false positives (number of individuals incorrectly classified as prone to show a behavior) for each true positive (person correctly identified as prone to exhibit a behavior) (NRC, 2003).[22] As this table shows, for a behavior that is seen in 10 percent of the population, even a test that correctly identifies 80 percent of those with a negative behavior (i.e., 80 percent sensitivity) and has 80 percent overall accuracy (i.e., overall proportion of true positives and true negatives identified by test) can be expected to incorrectly classify approximately four people as committing or being prone to commit the behavior for each one it correctly classifies.[23] The rarer the behavior and the less accurate the test, the greater the likelihood of incorrectly classifying someone as being prone to commit a behavior. Thus, many applicants who would not commit a negative behavior will be incorrectly classified as prone to commit the behavior. If employment decisions are based on this test, a large number of applicants would be excluded who would not commit the negative behavior of interest.

A recent study on the Air Force's Lackland Behavioral Questionnaire considered the extent to which the measure may assist in predicting relatively low-base-rate behaviors (Garb, Wirick, and Wood, 2012). One set of behaviors considered in this research involved criminal offenses, which has a base rate of 10.7 percent among enlisted Air Force personnel. This research demonstrated that, if those scoring in the most extreme 10 percent on the Lackland Behavioral Questionnaire were classified as likely to commit a criminal offense, approximately 21 percent of the individuals classified as such would be predicted to actually commit a crime. Notably, this measure was not designed solely to address the low-base-rate behaviors of criminal offenses. Rather, it considers a much broader set of negative behaviors (described previously); when all

Table 3.1. Number of People Incorrectly Classified for Every Person Correctly Classified (false positive index)

	Test Correctly Identifies											
	80% of Those with Negative Behavior				50% of Those with Negative Behavior				20% of Those with Negative Behavior			
Test accuracy (%)	90	80	70	60	90	80	70	60	90	80	70	60
Behavior present in												
1% of population	21.00	45.00	63.00	73.00	7.00	23.00	41.00	54.00	2.00	10.00	24.00	37.00
10% of population	1.90	4.10	5.70	6.70	0.63	2.10	3.70	4.90	0.18	0.94	2.20	3.30
50% of population	0.21	0.45	0.63	0.74	0.07	0.23	0.41	0.55	0.02	0.10	0.24	0.37

NOTE: Based on calculations from NRC (2003) calculations. Broadly, test accuracy may be considered an indication of the overall proportion of individuals who take a test who are correctly identified as having a negative behavior and correctly identified as not having a negative behavior.

---

[22] Values are based on the equivariance binomial model.

[23] Although they were the same in the described example, test sensitivity and accuracy are not always the same. An integrity test with much higher than 80 percent sensitivity or 80 percent test accuracy may be less feasible to develop.

these negative behaviors are considered together, the base rate for the behaviors is higher. In addition, the measure is not used to screen out individuals from the Air Force. Instead, it is used to determine whether further evaluation of these individuals is needed.

To address this issue of a test misclassifying a large number of individuals as prone to commit a negative behavior who would not actually commit the behavior, researchers have proposed implementing more than one preemployment screening test for a negative behavior (e.g., Martin, 1989). For example, one assessment or set of assessments might be used to classify individuals as prone or not prone to commit a behavior. Subsequent follow-up assessments might then also be used for this purpose. The number of false positives and false negatives might be lower if all measures classified an individual as either prone or not prone to commit the behavior. Notably, however, this process does not eliminate false positives and false negatives, particularly when attempting to address relative infrequent behaviors.

Sexual Assault Perpetration Estimates

As noted in the Section 1, this report draws from the UCMJ to define sexual assault. Recent RAND research grouped behaviors that fall under UCMJ sexual assault relevant offenses into three categories: penetrative sexual assault, nonpenetrative sexual assault, and attempted penetrative sexual assault (Morral, Gore, and Schell, 2015). Penetrative sexual assaults include penetration of the mouth, anus, or vagina by a penis, body part, or object. Nonpenetrative sexual assaults include incidents in which contact is made with the private areas of another person's body. Attempted penetrative sexual assault involves an event in which someone attempted to sexually assault another but did not make contact. These categories were used to establish the estimates we used at the beginning of Section 1, that 2.90 percent of active-duty women and 0.29 percent of active-duty men in the U.S. Air Force had experienced a sexual assault (Jaycox et al., 2015). This research and these estimates focused on sexual assault victims, not perpetrators, and parallel research addressing sexual assault perpetration in the U.S. military was not conducted.

Limited research is available that assesses sexual assault perpetration among U.S. military personnel. Previous research considering perpetration among U.S. Navy recruits found that 9.9 percent to 11.6 percent of those sampled had participated in premilitary rape (Merrill, Thomsen, et al., 2001; also see Merrill, Newell, et al., 1997). No estimates of sexual assault perpetration that are based on systematic research conducted across all the military services are available. Therefore, it is not clear what proportion of military personnel has committed sexual assault prior to or during their military service.

Although research has been conducted to establish estimates of sexual assault perpetration among nonmilitary personnel, different definitions and measures of sexual assault perpetration and use of nonrandom samples have contributed to different estimates of its prevalence. For example, researchers have noted that sexual assault estimates range from 7 percent to 57 percent (Abbey et al., 2001). Use of a definition of sexual assault that includes coercion (e.g., continual arguments) and not only force or threat of force can contribute to larger estimates of sexual assault (e.g., Spitzberg, 1999). In this report, sexual assault is conceptualized as those behaviors that are clearly punishable under the UCMJ. If the outcome behaviors of interest were expanded (e.g., include a range of sexually coercive behaviors), this would increase the base rate.

In addition, in this report, estimates of sexual assault perpetration are discussed in the context of employment screening and integrity testing research. Notably, employment screening and integrity testing research focus on counterproductive workplace behaviors, such as workplace violence. It is difficult to determine the prevalence of these behaviors, but researchers have considered certain counterproductive workplace behaviors, including workplace violence, to be infrequent (e.g., Dalton and Metzger, 1993; Grubb et al., 2005; Latham and Perlow, 1996; Murphy, 1987). Assertions that these are infrequent, or low-base-rate, behaviors tend to focus on the estimated proportion, not the number, of employees involved in the acts. For example, if 7 percent of employees engage in workplace violence, this may be considered a low base rate. However, an organization with 100,000 employees that had 7 percent of employees engaging in the negative acts would have 7,000 employees engaging, which might be considered a large number of employees.

As noted in Section 1, estimates of sexual assault perpetration are also difficult to establish. However, proportional estimates for certain counterproductive workplace behaviors, like workplace violence, are comparable to those for sexual assault perpetration involving military personnel (e.g., Budd, Arvey, and Lawless, 1996; Latham and Perlow, 1996; Merrill, Thomsen, et al., 2001). Thus, sexual assault perpetration may be considered to be at least as infrequent a behavior as certain other counterproductive workplace behaviors. That said, a potentially low base rate is not considered indicative of an acceptable or tolerable rate, particularly when discussing sexual assault perpetration.

Standards for Test Use

Addressing the related issues of low base rates and misclassification, Murphy (1987) provides two standards for the prediction of infrequent behaviors.[24] Based on his minimal threshold standard, when a negative behavior (e.g., theft, deception, or violence) is infrequent, the tendency of an integrity test to classify an innocent person as practicing this behavior should be equally infrequent. Thus, according to Murphy, the true positive rates of integrity tests should be equal to or greater than the false positive rates of these tests—a standard that integrity tests, and many other assessments, do not meet. His second standard is that of reasonable doubt. This standard would not exclude an applicant for employment unless the odds that the applicant will

---

[24] These standards are well known. However, as the additional discussion in this subsection shows, there are no widely accepted standards for the detection of infrequent behaviors.

perform a negative behavior are at least nine times as large as the odds that he or she will not doing so. Integrity tests are unlikely to meet this second standard.[25]

Sackett, Burris, and Callahan (1989), however, noted that Murphy does not account for selection ratio, or for the comparative nature of certain employment decisions. Specifically, Murphy does not address whether an employer is choosing from among a pool of applicants for a position or making a decision about employing a particular individual without comparison to others. If choosing from among a pool of applicants, and thus comparing one person or group to another, Murphy's standards may not apply. Sackett, Burris, and Callahan (1989, p. 522) noted:

> An employer with a single opening and two applicants, one with a test profile indicating a 10% likelihood of theft and the other with a test profile indicating a 20% likelihood of theft, may find that the reasonable doubt standard is not met for either but may conclude that test use to choose between applicants is rational. This is the essence of institutional prediction: in the long run the employer using the test will be better off than the employer choosing haphazardly, assuming test validity.

In this instance, integrity test scores may serve as one piece of information on a set of individuals that can help in choosing an employee or group of employees from a larger pool.

Many personnel-selection measures and procedures are probabilistic and may involve institutional prediction. That is, institutions would not use these measures to, for example, label a particular individual (e.g., as dishonest, aggressive, or lacking intelligence). Instead, they would use the measures to determine who may be more or less likely to succeed in the institution or who may be more or less likely to perform a negative behavior. These measures tend to be based on research demonstrating that the scores assist with differentiating applicants who are more or less likely to demonstrate certain behaviors. For example, previous research has shown that military enlistees without a high school diploma have an early attrition rate (i.e., during first six months of service) that is twice as high of those with a high school diploma (e.g., Buddin, 1984). The military has therefore established a high school diploma standard. Similarly, research has shown that individuals who obtain certain ASVAB scores perform better in various military occupations than those with lower scores (e.g., Ree, Earles, and Teachout, 1994), so these scores are used when making decisions regarding applicants.[26]

When using integrity tests to make a decision on the employment of a particular individual, not comparing his or her suitability to those of others who have also applied, Murphy's standards apply. In this situation, an employer is not comparing applicants and deciding which of the set is most likely to succeed or most likely to perform a negative behavior. Instead, the employer is

---

[25] Murphy (1987) assumes that psychologists use values of 0.95 or 0.99 for quantifying reasonable doubt in statistical hypothesis testing. For his purposes, he elects to use a more lenient 0.90. He notes "this 90% threshold for guilt requires posterior odds 9 times as large as the break-even threshold of one to one" (p. 612).

[26] Notably, neither of these standards or assessments is attempting to address an infrequent behavior, like theft or sexual assault. Research attempting to use measures to address low-base-rate behaviors should be expected to have great difficulty in differentiating between groups.

evaluating the qualifications of a single individual and determining whether that individual should be employed, regardless of who else has applied for a particular position in that organization. Sackett, Burris, and Callahan (1989, p. 522) noted:

> Assume an employer has administered an integrity test to a current employee, who has failed the test. In this case, a decision to terminate the employee would require that a very strong reasonable doubt standard be met.

Therefore, it can be difficult to demonstrate that integrity scores or other measures correctly classify a single individual as prone to conduct a behavior, particularly if that behavior has a low base rate. Thus, some scholars argue that these measures are inappropriate to label individuals and may be inappropriate to categorize them at all. However, if these scores are used comparatively and if research demonstrates that the scores differentiate between groups of applicants or employees in predicting certain outcomes, using the scores may be appropriate.

Discrimination and Privacy

Two additional issues that may arise during the use of integrity tests are their potential to discriminate against certain groups of individuals and their potential to be considered violations of applicants' privacy rights.

Title VII of the Civil Rights Act of 1964 prohibits employment discrimination in the civilian workforce on the basis of several categories. Currently protected categories are race, color, sex, religion, national origin, age, disability, and genetic information.[27] In prohibiting employment discrimination, Title VII forbids disparate impact, unless the practice or measure is job related and consistent with business necessity, and disparate treatment involving these categories or groups. *Disparate treatment* occurs when an employee (or group of employees) is intentionally treated differently from other similarly situated employees, and this treatment difference is based on the above-mentioned categories. In the case of integrity tests, disparate treatment might be present if, for example, only men were required to take the tests. In contrast, *disparate impact* occurs if an employer's policies or practices affect people in protected categories disproportionately, which may occur unintentionally. This would occur if, for example, scores on an integrity test disproportionately excluded certain groups (e.g., those of a certain race or ethnicity, men more than women). In this situation, the employer must demonstrate that this exclusion or selection policy is job related and consistent with business necessity (Equal Employment Opportunity Commission, 2010).

Some research on both overt and personality-based integrity tests has shown negligible differences in scores of different age, gender, racial, ethnic, and cultural groups (Fortmann and Leslie, 2003; Ones and Anderson, 2002; Ones and Viswesvaran, 1998). Research on other measures that are or may be used in personnel selection, but not considered to be integrity tests, have shown group differences (e.g., mean score differences). A great deal of research has been

---

[27] Also see the Rehabilitation Act of 1973 and the Genetic Information Nondiscrimination Act of 2008.

conducted on cognitive-ability tests. Although predictive of counterproductive workplace behaviors (e.g., Dilchert et al., 2007), cognitive-ability tests have shown group differences (see Roth et al., 2001). However, cognitive ability tests continue to be used because of their association with job-relevant behaviors. Further, a 2008 meta-analysis found several group differences between racial groups on certain facets of personality (Foldes, Duehr, and Ones, 2008). This suggests that measures used in personnel selection could adversely impact certain groups, depending on the measures used.

Privacy concerns are another issue that may arise when using integrity tests. Specifically, those who oppose employers' use of integrity tests claim that these measures invade applicants' and employees' privacy, because test items may address sensitive and personal topics for applicants (Metzger and Dalton, 1991). Privacy is protected by U.S. law (Restatement, Second, Torts § 652A-E, 1977). Integrity test items that are intrusive and not demonstrably related to an employer's needs and interests may be considered intrusions of employees' or applicants' rights to seclusion or privacy. Not all integrity tests invade privacy, but overt or personality-based integrity tests that contain items that specifically address physical or mental impairments may be subject to these concerns (Gutman, Koppes, and Vodanovich, 2011).

Title VII is not applied to the armed forces (*Roper v Department of the Army*, 832 F.2d 247, 248 [2d Cir. 1987]), but the employment discrimination issues it raises, particularly with regard to disparate impact, are worth military consideration (e.g., Goodell, 2010). Items regarding physical or mental impairments may be considered to address a legitimate organizational interest for the military. The armed forces should keep in mind extent to which items are of legitimate interest.

U.S. Military Personnel Selection and Classification Assessments

For decades, the U.S. military has explored the use of instruments for assisting with personnel selection and classification (Steinhaus and Waters, 1991). Two of these are the U.S. Army's Assessment of Background and Life Experiences (McHenry et al., 1990) and the U.S. Navy's Armed Services Applicant Profile (Trent and Quenette, 1992). As in nonmilitary settings, researchers and advisors for the U.S. military have expressed concerns about faking good and the potential for the security (e.g., scoring process, public availability) of these instruments to be compromised (Hough et al., 1990; also see Drasgow et al., 2012). U.S. military services have continued to use background checks and to explore the use of newly developed tests for screening and classification.

Background Checks

As noted earlier, to identify potentially disqualifying information, military applicants are asked to self-report information that may require moral-character waivers and to complete SF-86, Questionnaire for National Security Positions (see Section 2 for additional information on

Air Force screening). Previous research has shown that, across the U.S. military services, there are discrepancies between evidence of moral-character waivers and records of criminal convictions resulting from background checks (Buck and Neal, 2008). This research suggests that large numbers of individuals are not self-reporting previous criminal records that would require moral-character waivers. That is, applicants to the military services appear inclined to omit information that may lead the service to determine that they are unsuitable candidates. Instead, this information is often obtained during criminal-record checks performed after applicants complete the SF-86 form and waiver processing.

Tailored Adaptive Personality Assessment System

As noted in Section 2, the military services have begun to use TAPAS, a personality assessment that was originally developed for the U.S. Army (Drasgow et al., 2012; Nye et al., 2012). This assessment contains 21 facets of the Big Five personality traits and may expand to include additional facets of interest to the U.S. military (see Table 3.2).[28] It is designed to resist faking good and uses a forced-choice format, in which subsequent test items presented to individuals are based on their responses to earlier items (see Stark et al., 2012). Research has suggested minimal differences between gender and ethnic groups on different dimensions measured in TAPAS (Drasgow et al., 2012). Multiple versions of the TAPAS exist and are used to increase its security and utility.

Initial research suggests that TAPAS may help military occupational specialty (MOS) classification. Specifically, Nye et al. (2012) found that patterns across TAPAS scales differed across Army MOSs, suggesting that the TAPAS may help choose individuals for different MOSs (see also Drasgow et al., 2012). Nye et al. also found that TAPAS scales were significantly associated with job knowledge, Army Physical Fitness Test scores, disciplinary incidents, and attrition. Additional research has suggested that TAPAS can predict mental-disorder diagnosis and mental health-care utilization (Niebuhr et al., 2013).

TAPAS is relatively new, and most published research involving this assessment has used U.S. Army applicants and soldiers. Initial research with battlefield airmen and related specialties suggests that TAPAS has criterion-related validity when used with these groups (Rose, Manley, and Weissmuller, 2013). Additional research is needed to determine the instrument's utility across the services and across MOSs in the different services. Further, Murphy's (1987) standards may be relevant for considering whether to use TAPAS scores in deciding whether to admit or continue to employ individuals in the military. TAPAS is a broad personality measure and was not designed as an integrity test. However, it may include facets that are predictive of counterproductive workplace behaviors and could be used to design an integrity scale.

---

[28] When used, a particular version of TAPAS may contain fewer than 21 facets because the instrument becomes excessively long when a large number of facets are measured.

Table 3.2. Big Five Dimensions as Assessed by TAPAS

Big Five Dimension	TAPAS Facet	Brief Description
Extraversion	Dominance	High-scoring individuals are domineering, "take charge," and are often referred by their peers as "natural leaders."
	Sociability	High-scoring individuals tend to seek out and initiate social interactions.
	Attention seeking	High-scoring individuals tend to engage in behaviors that attract social attention; they are loud, entertaining, and even boastful.
Agreeableness	Consideration	Individuals scoring high on this facet are affectionate, compassionate, sensitive, and caring.
	Generosity	High-scoring individuals are generous with their time and resources.
	Cooperation	High-scoring individuals are pleasant, trusting, cordial, noncritical, and easy to get along with.
Conscientiousness	Achievement	High-scoring individuals are seen as hard working, ambitious, confident, and resourceful.
	Order	High-scoring individuals tend to organize tasks and activities and desire to maintain neat and clean surroundings.
	Self-control	High-scoring individuals tend to be cautious, levelheaded, able to delay gratification, and patient.
	Responsibility	High-scoring individuals are dependable, reliable, and make every effort to keep their promises.
	Nondelinquency	High-scoring individuals tend to comply with rules, customs, norms, and expectations, and they tend not to challenge authority.
	Virtue	High-scoring individuals strive to adhere to standards of honesty, morality, and "good Samaritan" behavior.
Emotional stability	Adjustment	High-scoring individuals are well adjusted, worry free, and handle stress well.
	Even tempered	High-scoring individuals tend to be calm and stable. They don't often exhibit anger, hostility, or aggression.
	Optimism	High-scoring individuals have a positive outlook on life and tend to experience joy and a sense of well-being.
Openness to experience	Intellectual efficiency	High-scoring individuals are able to process information quickly and would be described by others as knowledgeable, astute, and intellectual.
	Ingenuity	High-scoring individuals are inventive and think "outside of the box."
	Curiosity	High-scoring individuals are inquisitive and perceptive, they are interested in learning new information and attend courses and workshops whenever they can.
	Aesthetics	High-scoring individuals appreciate various forms of art and music and participate in art-related activities more often than others.
	Tolerance	High-scoring individuals scoring are interested in other cultures and opinions that may differ from their own.
	Depth	High-scoring individuals exhibit behaviors targeted toward understanding the meaning of one's life and/or facilitating self-improvement, reflection, and self-actualization.
Not applicable	Physical conditioning	High-scoring individuals tend to engage in activities to maintain their physical fitness and are more likely participate in vigorous sports or exercise.

NOTE: Table used with permission from Stark et al., 2014.

Researchers have proposed that several characteristics may be associated with sexual assault perpetration, and TAPAS assesses many of these proposed characteristics (see Greathouse et al.,

2015; Malamuth et al., 1995; Malamuth, 1996; Tharp et al., 2012). These characteristics include narcissism and dominance (opposite of consideration), self-control (opposite of impulsivity), responsibility and nondelinquency (opposite of delinquency), and even-temperedness (opposite of aggression). TAPAS could be one measure to use in validation research involving sexual assault proclivity.

Additional Measures

Previous research and theory suggest that aggressive and hostile tendencies may be associated with proclivity to perpetrate sexual assault (e.g., Malamuth et al., 1995). This section briefly reviews information on and measurements of workplace aggression and sexual aggression. It also discusses possible aspects to consider in applying measures of aggression for applicant and employee selection and screening. The previously described integrity tests have traditionally been used to address deception and workplace theft (Sackett, Burris, and Callahan, 1989).Workplace violence is rarely the sole focus of integrity tests or other self-report measures (e.g., Hough and Oswald, 2000; Martinko, Gundlach, and Douglas, 2002; Ones, Viswesvaran, and Schmidt, 1993), making it difficult to assess the value of these measures for addressing workplace violence. Other measures have been developed to assess respondent levels of sexual aggression and likelihood to conduct sexual assault (see Greathouse et al., 2015, for a detailed review of measures of sexual assault). However, the predictive validity of these measures has not been established, and they were not developed to identify the likelihood that an applicant for employment will commit sexual assault.

Measures of Workplace Aggression

Workplace aggression and violence are not interchangeable; rather, violence (e.g., physical assaults) may be considered one of many forms of aggression (i.e., any behavior intended to cause physical or psychological harm). Acts of workplace violence can thus be considered acts of workplace aggression, but not all acts of workplace aggression are acts of violence (Barling, Dupré, and Kelloway, 2009).[29] Most research in this area has focused on factors associated with aggression rather than on correlates of violence specifically. As noted earlier, relatively little recent research has considered the use of tests for predicting workplace aggression or violence.

Factors Associated with Workplace Aggression

Research on predictors of workplace aggression suggests that higher trait anger (i.e., a disposition in which one frequently experiences anger), more positive attitudes toward revenge, a hostile attribution style (i.e., attribution of negative workplace outcomes to external, stable, intentional, and controllable causes), a hostile personality style (e.g., impatient and irritable), and

---

[29] There is less agreement on the differentiation between sexual violence and sexual aggression. For example, sexual violence may reference aggression (Basile et al., 2014).

masculinity are individual characteristics associated with higher incidence of workplace aggression (Douglas and Martinko, 2001; Hammock and Richardson, 1992; Hershcovis et al., 2007; Neuman and Baron, 1998). Different measures exist to address these constructs and may be considered for addressing aggressive applicants and employees. Examples of such measures include

- anger: State-Trait Anger Expression Inventory 2, (Spielberger, 1999)
- attitudes toward revenge: Vengeance Scale (Stuckless and Goranson, 1992)
- hostile attribution style: Organizational Attributional Style Questionnaire (Kent and Martinko, 1995)
- hostile personality style: Buss-Perry Aggression Questionnaire (Buss and Perry, 1992)
- masculinity: Bem Sex-Role Inventory (Bem, 1974).

Several negative life events, such as criminal activity; negative workplace events, such as a decrease in earnings over time; and drug use are also associated with workplace aggression (Fletcher, Brakel, and Cavanaugh, 2000; Sarchione et al., 1998).

Individuals with higher levels of exhaustion and lower levels of job satisfaction may be more likely to participate in acts of workplace aggression (Blau and Andersson, 2005). Additional factors associated with workplace aggression include perceived workplace injustice (e.g., unfairness of outcomes), the presence of constraints preventing an individual from performing assigned tasks (e.g., lack of available resources), interpersonal conflict, and poor leadership (Douglas and Martinko, 2001; Greenberg and Algae, 1998; Hershcovis et al., 2007). In short, multiple individual-level characteristics and situational factors are associated with workplace aggression.

Assessing Proclivity for Aggression

Most research on proclivity for aggression has relied on information obtained through self-reports. Recently, researchers have suggested that aggressive tendencies should not be assessed through traditional measures involving self-report information because individuals may be unable to provide accurate information on unconscious aggressive cognitions (Burroughs and James, 2005). The Conditional Reasoning Test for Aggression (CRT-A), which assumes that those who have aggressive tendencies are likely to find statements that justify aggression to be more persuasive than other statements, seeks to overcome this problem. It builds from research on conditional reasoning tests (see LeBreton et al., 2007). CRT-A participants are presented with a series of statements and asked to identify which is most persuasive. Individuals finding the statements justifying aggression to be more logical or persuasive than passive or neutral statements are considered to have a greater proclivity for aggression. Although initial research suggested the CRT-A was a valid predictor of aggression, later research suggested that this measure has lower validity than initial estimates suggested but that its validity is comparable to those of integrity tests (Berry, Sackett, and Tobares, 2010; Burroughs and James, 2005). Additional measures of proclivity for aggression may be worthwhile to consider.

Addressing Aggression in the Workplace

Fletcher, Brakel, and Cavenaugh (2000), in their review of workplace violence in the United States, proposed several measures that employers may take to assess an individual's likelihood to engage in workplace aggression and violence. In describing the profile of a violent person, they note:

> One of the best predictors of future violence is a history of violence, with an increase in potential with each prior act of aggression. Other research has shown aggression to be a relatively stable characteristic. External factors such as recent termination or lay-off may cause the perpetrator to act aggressively and/or violently. Other factors that increase the potential for violence include alcohol or drug misuse and the availability of guns. Alcohol misuse has been linked to an increased likelihood that the user will "misread" situations, and has been shown to increase impulsivity.

As part of preemployment screening evaluations, these researchers recommend a thorough interview that addresses previous interactions or relationships with employers, relationships with friends and family, and criminal history. If issues involving personality, interpersonal functioning, or substance use are found during the preemployment interview, additional psychological tests may be pursued. For current employees identified as potentially at risk for displaying aggression or violence, a review of previous work history, more-recent work incidents, and situational factors (e.g., marital conflict, shift change) can help evaluate fitness for duty. Notably, the extent to which interviews assist in addressing aggression, above and beyond other measures (e.g., TAPAS) and current backgrounds checks, requires further assessment among Air Force personnel. These interviews should be expected to suffer from many of the same issues as other preemployment measures, including integrity tests, when classifying individuals based on behaviors with low base rates.

Measures of Sexual Aggression Proclivity

Relatively little research has addressed the specific topic of testing for the prevention of sexual assault among employees. Researchers addressing workplace behaviors tend to reference general assault and note that sexual harassment may be considered to be a form of workplace aggression (Fletcher, Brakel and Cavanaugh, 2000; Lieber, 2007; Schneider, 2001). Perhaps because of the potentially low rate of sexual assault among employees, no well-validated and widely used test for sexual assault prevention in the workplace is currently available (see Greathouse et al., 2015, for a detailed review of measures of sexual assault). However, various measures designed to assess sexual harassment and sexual assault have been developed, and previous research has considered cognitive factors that may be associated with sexually coercive behaviors (Drieschner and Lange, 1999; Malamuth et al., 1995; Tharp et al., 2012; Thompson et al., 2011; also see Greathouse et al., 2015).

Measures of Sexual Harassment

Research involving military personnel suggests that women who are sexually harassed are 14 times more likely to be sexually assaulted than women who are not sexually harassed, and men who are sexually harassed are 49 times more likely to be sexually assaulted than men who are not sexually harassed (Farris et al., 2015). We therefore consider measures of sexual harassment and what they may indicate about perpetration of sexual assault in the military.

Pryor (1987) developed the Likelihood to Sexually Harass Scale, and Bingham and Burleson (1996) later developed a Sexual Harassment Proclivity Scale. Both scales appear to be moderately correlated with attitudinal variables that may be relevant to sexual harassment; the Likelihood to Sexually Harass Scale also appears to be related to relevant behavioral variables involving harassment (see Pina, Gannon, and Saunders, 2009). Additional potential measures of interest for predicting sexual harassment include authoritarianism and hostile sexism. Authoritarianism involves adherence to social norms, submission to established persons or institutions of authority, and aggression against those who challenge norms and established authority (Altemeyer, 1996). Hostile sexism involves hostility or aggression toward women (Glick and Fiske, 1996). Research has shown that higher levels of authoritarianism are associated with higher likelihood to sexually harass, and hostile sexism mediates the relationship between these constructs (i.e., serves as a connecting variable between the constructs; Begany and Milburn, 2002). Similar research with U.S. Air Force noncommissioned officers has shown that greater hostile sexism among BMT instructors is positively associated with maltreatment of female trainees and negatively associated with student evaluations of trainers (Barron and Ogle, 2014).

This initial research seems to suggest one potential direction for reducing incidents of sexual harassment in the workforce. Specifically, organizations may consider measuring likelihood or proclivity to sexually harass or hostile sexism and subsequent selection of individuals with comparatively low scores on these measures for positions that require extended interactions with subordinates (e.g., trainers and recruiters). However, no known research has thoroughly examined the effects of using these measures for personnel screening and selection. The purpose of these measures is likely to be clear to respondents (example item: "Women are too easily offended" [Glick and Fiske, 1996]). As such, the measures may be highly susceptible to faking good and may elicit negative reactions from offended respondents. Initial research with these and related measures has focused on sexual harassment, so the applicability of these measures for preventing sexual assault among employees is less clear. Only limited initial research suggests that hostile sexism may be associated with rape proclivity (Masser, Viki, and Power, 2006). High scores on these measures do not indicate that an individual will engage in sexual harassment. Thus, they may be inappropriate to use when deciding whether to hire or maintain employment of a particular individual.

Measures of Sexual Assault

Focusing more specifically on sexual assault, several measures have sought to assess rape proclivity or the likelihood of engaging in sexual assault. Most of these measures focus on male-on-female sexual assault. To assess sexual assault, Malamuth and his colleagues used two single-item measures asking men to indicate, if they were not caught, the likelihood they would (1) rape and (2) force a woman to do something she did not really want to do (1 = *not at all likely,* 5 = *very likely*; Briere and Malamuth, 1983; Malamuth, 1981). Each measure involves only one item (Malamuth, 1988). Thus, the reliability of these measures is questionable. Koss and Oros (1982) also developed a measure of naturalistic sexual aggression that is designed to address hidden cases of rape (i.e., those not reported). Revised versions of this instrument are frequently used in research on sexual aggression.[30] Some other measures that may be associated with rape proclivity include hostility toward women, acceptance of violence against women, antisocial personality characteristics, and desires to sexually dominate a victim (Malamuth, 1986).

All these measures may be considered to have an overt purpose. Specifically, participants are likely to know why a current or potential employer is asking these items. As with overt purpose integrity tests, these measures are likely to be susceptible to faking good and have the potential to offend participants. As noted with measures of sexual harassment, individuals with high scores on these measures will not necessarily engage in sexual assault against another person. Building from Murphy's (1987) standards, these tests may be inappropriate to use in determining whether to hire a particular individual.[31] However, if the susceptibility of measures of sexual assault to faking can be reduced, these measures may assist when choosing among a pool of individuals for particular positions. Another potential issue associated with these tests is that, if administered to all of those under consideration in employment decisions, they may adversely affect certain applicants or employees, such as adversely affecting men more than women.

Current Air Force Personnel Center Research Effort

In FY 2014, AFPC began assessments to develop and evaluate a screening tool to identify risk of sexual assault perpetration among Air Force applicants and personnel. These assessments were ongoing at the time of this research, and RAND has not evaluated them. However, information provided in this report may help inform these efforts.

One of the AFPC assessments has involved examining archival records of enlisted accessions from 2006 to 2013 to determine whether current measures the Air Force administers are associated with sexual assault charges and convictions listed in the Defense Incident-Based Reporting System. Another assessment AFPC is conducting has involved examining the associations between anonymous self-report admissions among BMT trainees of past sexual

---

[30] This self-report measure may suffer from misleading participant responses (i.e., faking good).

[31] These standards are well known, but there are no widely accepted standards for the detection of infrequent behaviors.

assault, including using physical force to obtain sex, and past sexual coercion, including using intoxication or verbal coercion to obtain sex, prior to joining the Air Force and future intent to sexually harass (e.g., give applicant a job in exchange for sexual favors, without concern of repercussion) with trainees' responses to several other measures. Three percent of males and 1 percent of females indicated that they had used physical force or intoxication to obtain sex (e.g., "Have you ever had sexual intercourse with someone, even though they did not want to, because they were too intoxicated to resist your sexual advances?"). Approximately 27 percent of males and 10 percent of females indicated that they had used some form of verbal coercion to obtain sex (e.g., "Have you ever obtained sexual intercourse by making someone think you cared for them more than you really did?").[32]

Summary

This section considered the use of integrity tests and other measures for screening potential sexual assault perpetrators. Integrity tests tend to be paper-and-pencil or computer-based instruments that businesses and organizations use to predict job performance and counterproductive workplace behaviors. Overt integrity tests directly assess attitudes about counterproductive thoughts and actions. Personality-based tests use measures of personality dimensions to predict counterproductive behaviors. Research generally suggests that overt and personality-based integrity tests are valid predictors of job performance and counterproductive behaviors. However, the ability of these tests to predict behaviors of interest may vary by measurement method, the breadth of the measure, and the group that is tested. These tests also have limitations, including susceptibility to faking good and misclassification.

Two additional concerns about the use of integrity tests are whether they adversely affect certain groups and whether they invade employees' or applicants' privacy. Several studies demonstrated negligible differences between different groups on integrity test scores, but additional research suggests that, depending on which integrity test measures are used, they may adversely affect certain groups. Thus, consideration should be given to the extent that measures addressing sexual harassment or assault adversely affect certain groups (e.g., men). In addition, although not all integrity tests are considered to invade individual privacy, certain tests are suspect. Thus, questioning individuals about sexual experiences may be considered an invasion of privacy and should require approval from appropriate legal entities and pretesting with applicants or potential applicants.

Integrity tests have traditionally been used to predict job performance and counterproductive workplace behavior. Other tests may help address workplace aggression or workplace violence. However, these constructs are rarely the sole focus of an integrity test or of research validating

---

[32] These differing proportions, based on the behavior assessed, demonstrate how the operationalization of sexual assault can affect the observed base rate.

an integrity test (e.g., Ones, Viswesvaran, and Schmidt, 1993). This makes it difficult to assess the utility of broad integrity tests for addressing these narrow aspects of workplace relations. Additional measures have been developed to assess respondent levels of sexual aggression and likelihood to conduct sexual assault, but the predictive validity of these measures is questionable. Perhaps because of the potentially low rate of sexual assault among employees (or the low rate of reports of sexual assault), no well-validated and widely used test for identifying potential sexual assault perpetrators in the workplace is currently available.

One option organizations may consider is measures that may be associated with sexual assault (e.g., antisocial personality characteristics and the desire to sexually dominate a victim) as one point of information, particularly for positions requiring extensive interaction with subordinates and a great deal of autonomy. These measures may be used as part of system for selecting among employees applying for a position within an organization, such as trainer or recruiter, so those with higher scores on these measures would be less likely to be selected for these roles. TAPAS may also be worth considering because it addresses several dimensions that are believed to be associated with sexually aggressive behaviors. Before being used for such purposes, the measures would need to be validated, using individuals from the population of interest. Moreover, the potential challenges of using these measures, including faking good, misclassification, disparate impact, and privacy concerns, would need to be considered and addressed.

4. Conclusions and Recommendations

This report considered whether certain screening may help identify individuals who may have a greater likelihood of perpetrating sexual assault in the Air Force. To do so, the report reviewed the current Air Force policies and procedures for prescreening and prequalification of Air Force applicants. It also reviewed research on integrity tests, background checks, and additional measures and considered the applicability of these measures for addressing sexual assault in the workplace. This section summarizes preliminary recommendations that draw from this information.

Prescreening to Address Sexual Assault Perpetration

AFRS takes a series of actions during the recruitment process to disqualify individuals with certain characteristics. No analyses have been conducted that assess how these actions affect the potential of Air Force applicants and enlistees to perpetuate sexual assault. However, current Air Force policies and actions may prevent those who have a greater likelihood to commit sexual assault in the future from joining the Air Force.

During optional preliminary screening of an individual interested in the Air Force, a recruiter may determine that the person has a history of antisocial behavior, so the recruiter may decline to schedule a formal appointment with the applicant. If not eliminated from consideration during an optional preliminary screening, an applicant may volunteer information regarding a history of perpetration during the prescreening process at a formal appointment with a recruiter or during the prequalification and prescreening procedures that primarily take place at USMEPCOM. These procedures do not include explicit questions about whether an individual was ever charged with, has ever been accused of, or ever perpetrated a sexual assault. The Air Force may wish to ask about these behaviors explicitly during prescreening interviews. During prescreening, applicants are also informed of behaviors considered to be professional and unprofessional between applicants and recruiters, which begins the process of conveying Air Force norms for appropriate behavior.

After passing through the prescreening and prequalification processes, an applicant must complete the security-investigation process. This process involves a thorough review of an applicant's history, which may uncover a history of rape or sexual assault perpetration. If disqualifications are identified during the prescreening or security investigation processes, an applicant may ask to pursue a waiver. Waivers for individuals convicted of sexual assault, however, are highly unlikely.

Applicability of Various Measures for Sexual Assault Prevention

Integrity tests and other measures may be used to assist with screening applicants to the Air Force or for screening those currently in the Air Force who are applying for certain positions within the service. Research on integrity testing suggests that these tests may help predict applicant and employee job performance and counterproductive workplace behaviors. These tests and similar measures are susceptible to faking good, such that individuals can provide responses that are likely to make them appear to be more suitable employees. New measures, such as those using forced-choice formats, appear to be more resistant, but not completely immune, to faking good. Further, the use of integrity tests and similar measures for determining whether to hire or maintain employment of a particular individual may not meet minimal threshold or reasonable-doubt standards, particularly when used to detect low-base-rate behaviors. However, using these to help choose an employee from a pool of applicants for a position is more promising.

Compared to the use of integrity tests for assessing job performance, deception, or workplace theft, research on the use of measures for assessing likelihood of perpetrating workplace violence, sexual harassment, and sexual assault is more limited. Various measures have been developed to address each of these constructs, but these measures may also suffer from faking good. They may also be inappropriate to use when deciding whether to accept a particular candidate for Air Force service. The association between high scores on these measures and future participation in aggressive or violent acts is not well established, and misclassification of individuals may be highly likely.

Recommendations

Drawing from the information summarized above, RAND developed initial recommendations that may assist the Air Force in addressing and communicating the service's lack of tolerance for sexual assault to applicants and current employees. These recommendations address changes that the service may make to its current preemployment screening practices and changes that may be incorporated into the selection process for certain positions in the Air Force.

The Air Force application process has at least two potential ways to address sexual assault prevention. One involves conveying norms for appropriate behavior in the Air Force to applicants. Thus, individuals who would not appreciate the Air Force's intolerance for sexual assault can self-select out of the process. Further, individuals who may have a propensity to commit assault in lenient situations (e.g., Malamuth, 1981) would be given normative information that the Air Force is not lenient toward sexual assault, thereby potentially deterring behaviors in which some might otherwise engage. The second is to exclude people who volunteer, admit to, or are found out to have a history of perpetrating sexual assault.

Provide Additional Information to Applicants on Air Force Intolerance of Sexual Assault

When providing applicants with information on professional and unprofessional behaviors in the service, the Air Force should communicate its intolerance of sexual assault. As part of the ID3A, recruiters are responsible for communicating the guidelines for appropriate recruiter-applicant interactions. This is outlined in the AFRS Commander Professional Relationship video, ID3A Rights/Responsibilities card, and ID3A Video Slide and Talking Points. When applicants are receiving this information, the Air Force should provide additional information to applicants about sexual assault. Specifically, applicants should receive detailed information on the Air Force's cultural intolerance of sexual assault, which may include the definition of sexual assault and ways the Air Force addresses sexual assault and how applicants and Air Force personnel can address the subject (e.g., Butler, 2012).

Further, individuals provided this information should be required to review and demonstrate understanding of it. Individuals may demonstrate knowledge, or understanding, by responding to a variety of questions following information presentation. These questions can ask individuals to explain the difference between sexual assault and consensual sex and how they should report sexual assault if they see or experience it (Driscoll, 2000). To demonstrate immediate knowledge, these questions may be asked immediately after the presentation (Kirkpatrick, 2006). To demonstrate retention of information, questions may be asked two to three weeks following the presentation (Driskell, Willis, and Copper, 1992).

Providing information and programming that educates individuals on sexual assault has been recommended for preventing sexual offenses (Lee et al., 2003). Some research suggests that providing this information may help prevent sexual assault (Anderson and Whitson, 2005; Rothman and Silverman, 2007). By presenting information on sexual assault and the Air Force's intolerance of it early in the application process, the service can quickly begin a sustained prevention effort that clearly communicates the service's attitude toward and response to sexual assault. To determine the effectiveness of providing this information, an evaluation should be conducted.[33]

Ask Applicants Questions on History of Sexual Assault Perpetration

Although the literature has identified a number of risk factors for sexual assault have been identified, previous sexual assault behavior appears to be the strongest available predictor of

---

[33] To assess the effectiveness of providing this specific information, it would first be necessary to gather all the information shared with applicants and ensure that it is standardized—what is shown, how it is shown, to whom, by whom, and when. It would then be necessary to assess participants' knowledge, attitudes, and behavioral inclinations before and immediately after exposure to this information, perhaps through surveys. Ideally, there would also be a control group, which would not receive the information but would also take the survey. The evaluation would them compare the responses of those who had received the information against those of the control group. In addition, to examine the impact of providing this information over time, participants' knowledge, attitudes, and behaviors may also be measured repeatedly.

future behavior (Loh et al., 2005). To address sexual assault behaviors, it is worthwhile to obtain relevant information as early as possible. Thus, the Air Force should obtain more information on an applicant's sexually aggressive behavioral history early in the application process. The Air Force has a moral eligibility determination requirement for applicants who admit to or are charged with but not have not been convicted or adversely adjudicated for offenses requiring a waiver, including rape (AFRS Instruction 36-3001, 2012). To increase the opportunities for applicants to provide information regarding sexually aggressive behavior, the Air Force should ask applicants about their history of sexual assault perpetration during the prescreening or prequalification of applicants. A standardized, explicit question or set of questions on conviction for sexual assault or on performance of sexual assault behaviors even without conviction would help the Air Force conduct a more through initial review of applicants. If an applicant provides an affirmative response on prior sexually aggressive behavior, the Air Force may, at a minimum, require completion of a moral eligibility determination that must be reviewed by at least a squadron commander. Use of multiple instruments may help better determine the risks an applicant presents for perpetrating sexual assault. Alternatively, assessments addressing this behavior may be conducted at MEPS, which may also help ensure that assessments are consistent and standardized.

To implement this new request for information, the forms that applicants, recruiters, the MEPS LNCO, and USMEPCOM currently complete could include questions addressing relevant topics from the well-known Sexual Experiences Survey (Koss et al., 2006) or a small set of modified questions on the perpetration of acts described in the 2014 RAND Military Workplace Survey (Morral, Gore, and Schell, 2014). More specifically, one example question that draws from recommended measures for soliciting self-reports of sexual aggression and the definition of rape that Air Force recruiting uses (AFRS Instruction 36-3001, 2012; Koss et al., 2006) is: "Did you ever have sex with someone when they didn't want to, or when they were asleep, unconscious, or too out of it to stop it? By sex, we are including oral, anal, and vaginal sex."[34] Additionally, the Air Force could ask whether applicants have been charged with or convicted of sexual assault when asking about charges and convictions for other crimes. Although they already receive questions about their medical history, legal history, substance use, and past delinquent behaviors, some applicants may consider inquiries into their history of sexual assault perpetration to be violations of privacy, so this should only be considered if approved by the appropriate parties, including legal entities, in the Air Force. Even if approved, pretesting should be conducted to determine on how this questioning on applicant, or potential applicant, affects perceptions of the Air Force and inclinations to join the Air Force. At a minimum, asking for this information will help communicate to applicants the Air Force's lack of tolerance for sexual

---

[34] The Air Force may consider including one or two less-threatening questions on sexual experience before asking applicants about their history of sexual aggression or sexual assault perpetration. For example, rather than immediately asking applicants about sexually aggressive behaviors, a question addressing whether an applicant has ever had any kind of sexual experience could be asked first.

assault and its interest in removing from consideration those who have participated in this behavior. Further, requesting this information may help quickly identify and disqualify applicants who have engaged in these acts.

Notably, individuals may omit information from self-reports, as previous research on moral waivers and background checks in the military services suggest. The Air Force may consider more-thorough background checks that specifically assess an individual's history of sexual assault and aggression. To collect information for a background check, an applicant's security clearance screening (e.g., in the SF-86) may include additional questions, but this would require coordination with and approval from multiple federal entities (e.g., the Office of Personnel Management's Federal Investigative Services). Alternatively, the Air Force would need to conduct additional background checks beyond those already conducted for security clearances.[35] Both options would require extensive time and resources and should only be pursued after approval from the appropriate parties, including legal entities, and pretesting with applicants or potential applicants to the Air Force.

Use Well-Validated Measures to Select Individuals

The utility of various tests for addressing workplace violence or sexual aggression remains unclear. When deciding between individuals for a position, particularly those that involve frequent interaction with subordinates (e.g., recruiter or trainer), the Air Force should use measures that address sexual assault proclivity or factors related to this proclivity to choose from a pool of applicants. No current measure developed for employment screening is both clearly related to likelihood of sexual assault and not easily susceptible to faking good. Development of such a measure or a combination of such measures would assist with selecting from among a pool of potential individuals who are likely to interact with vulnerable subordinates frequently. For example, all else being relatively equal, individuals who score lower on such measures may be better suited for positions as trainers, recruiters, or others who interact frequently with subordinates. Developing a measure that is both clearly related to likelihood of sexual assault and not easily susceptible to faking will require time and resources.

To assist with development, the Air Force should assess the validity of tests, such as TAPAS, for predicting sexual assault behaviors. These assessments should use samples of individuals from the population to which the tests will be applied. For example, if the tests are to be administered to and used to select individuals who are currently in the Air Force, these validity assessments should sample individuals who are currently in the Air Force. If the assessments are to be used to screen Air Force applicants, the validity assessments should sample Air Force applicants.

---

[35] The Air Force currently conducts a less-formal local law violation request, a check with a national or local agency, and an Office of Personnel Management's Federal Investigative Services background check.

Validation studies for potential sexual assault screening measures can involve assessment of criterion-related validity, which examines whether there is an association between the measure and the criterion, or outcome, of interest. Studies examining criterion-related validity may use predictive methodology, involving data collection at different times, or concurrent methodology, involving data collection at the same time. Although no assessment is without limitations (e.g., see Hall, 1990), criterion-related validity assessments that may be considered include a prospective study involving Air Force personnel or applicants (e.g., Thompson et al., 2011), a longitudinal study involving Air Force personnel or applicants (e.g., Abbey and McAuslan, 2004), and examination of the association between responses of Air Force applicants or personnel to these measures and their responses about previous sexual assault behavior or their responses about the extent to which they would conduct sexual assault if there were no chance of being caught (e.g., see Drieschner and Lange, 1999). This assessment may therefore entail examining the association of scores on an integrity test administered at one time with later behavior, or it may involve examining the associations between responses to assessments that are administered at the same time.

Additional assessments may also be conducted, including studies that consider content validity (the extent to which a test measures the construct of interest). These may compare responses of those convicted for sexual assault in the Air Force with a random sample of Air Force personnel or applicants (e.g., Malamuth, 1981). The Air Force should also assess the extent to which these measures may lead to misclassification, including false positives and false negatives (e.g., NRC, 2003).

During development of and extensive research on an employment screening measure or set of measures that are clearly related to likelihood of sexual assault, the Air Force may consider using measures that are more weakly associated with sexual assault proclivity. These include antisocial personality characteristics and desire to sexually dominate a victim (also see Greathouse et al., 2015). Scores on one or a combination of measures may help the service with evaluate a person's suitability for a position (e.g., recruiter or trainer) relative to others who have also applied for the position. For example, all else being equal, the service can select the person with lower scores on a measure of antisocial personality characteristics when choosing between two applicants for a position. As described previously, these measures are likely susceptible to faking good, and additional research would need to assess the strength of their association with rape proclivity and, hence, their validity for this purpose. Therefore, before wide-scale implementation, the tests need to be validated using information from individuals who belong to the population of interest. The tests should not be the only or most heavily weighted piece of information for evaluating applicants for a position. Scores on these measures should also never be used to label someone based on sexual assault proclivity. Grouping or classifying individuals based on these scores runs the risk of individuals being labeled based on their presumed proclivity.

The Air Force may want to use employment-screening measures to screen out applicants to the service who may be more likely to conduct sexual assault. If implementing these measures during applicant screening, the Air Force will need to balance the cost of screening individuals out (and potentially increasing recruiting efforts) against the potential benefit of preventing an offender.

Conclusion

As part of its sexual assault-prevention efforts, the Air Force may modify its current policies and procedures for preemployment and position screening to better address the potential for sexual assault perpetration. No existing integrity tests are clearly and strongly associated with an individual's likelihood to conduct sexual assault. No off-the-shelf measure exists for identifying individuals who are highly prone to perpetrate sexual assault that the Air Force can adopt at this time. This report considered alternative options for the Air Force to pursue for addressing sexual assault during employment screening.

Current Air Force policies and procedures may help prevent sexual assault in the service. By making some changes to current policies and practices, the Air Force may further improve its sexual assault prevention efforts. These changes may include presenting service applicants with information on the Air Force's intolerance for sexual assault, prescreening that addresses an applicant's previous sexual assault behavior more thoroughly, and development and inclusion of measures related to sexual assault proclivity for use in the selection process for certain Air Force positions.

Appendix A: Example Moral Offenses

- Example Category 1 offenses
  - Aggravated assault with a dangerous weapon, intentionally inflicting great bodily harm, with intent to commit a felony (adjudicated as an adult only)
  - Bribery (adjudicated as an adult only)
  - Burglary (adjudicated as an adult only)
  - Carnal knowledge of a child under 16 years of age
  - Extortion (adjudicated as an adult only)
  - Indecent acts or liberties with a child under 16 years of age, molestation
  - Kidnapping, abduction
  - Manslaughter (includes voluntary and vehicular)
  - Murder
  - Perjury (adjudicated as an adult only)
  - Rape
  - Robbery (adjudicated as an adult only)

- Example Category 2 offenses
  - Aggravated assault with a dangerous weapon, intentionally inflicting great bodily harm, with intent to commit a felony (adjudicated as a juvenile only)
  - Arson
  - Attempting to commit a felony
  - Breaking and entering a building with the intent to commit a felony
  - Bribery (adjudicated as a juvenile only)
  - Burglary (adjudicated as a juvenile only)
  - Carrying a concealed firearm or unlawful carrying of a firearm
  - Child pornography offenses
  - Conspiring to commit a felony
  - Criminal libel
  - DUI or DWI: driving under the influence of, or while intoxicated or impaired by, alcohol or drugs
  - Embezzlement
  - Extortion (adjudicated as a juvenile only)
  - Forgery: knowingly uttering or passing a forged instrument (except for altered identification for purchase of alcoholic beverages)
  - Grand larceny
  - Grand theft
  - Housebreaking
  - Indecent assault
  - Involuntary manslaughter
  - Leaving the scene of an accident (hit and run) involving personal injury

- Looting
- Mail or electronic emission matters: abstracting, destroying, obstructing, opening, secreting, stealing, or taking
- Mail: depositing obscene or indecent matter (including electronic or computerized email or bulletin board systems)
- Maiming or disfiguring
- Marijuana: simple possession or use
- Negligent homicide
- Pandering
- Prostitution or soliciting to commit prostitution
- Public record: altering, concealing, destroying, mutilating, obliterating, or removing
- Riot
- Selling, leasing, or transferring a weapon to a minor or unauthorized individual
- Sexual harassment
- Willfully discharging firearms so as to endanger life or shooting in public place

- Example Category 3 offenses

    - Assault (simple)
    - Breaking and entering a vehicle
    - Carrying a concealed weapon (other than firearm), possession of brass knuckles
    - Check: insufficient funds (amount more than $50, worthless, or uttering with intent to defraud or deceive)
    - Conspiring to commit a misdemeanor
    - Contempt of court (including nonpayment of child support or alimony required by court order)
    - Contributing to the delinquency of a minor (including purchase of alcoholic beverages)
    - Desecration of a grave
    - Discharging a firearm through carelessness or within municipal limits
    - Drunk in public, drunk and disorderly, public intoxication
    - Failure to stop and render aid after an accident
    - Indecent exposure
    - Indecent, insulting, or obscene language communicated directly or by telephone
    - Killing a domestic animal
    - Leaving the scene of an accident involving no personal injury
    - Liquor or alcoholic beverages: unlawful manufacture or sale
    - Malicious mischief
    - Removing property under lien or from public grounds
    - Resisting, fleeing, or eluding arrest
    - Shooting from a highway or on public road
    - Shoplifting, larceny, petty larceny, theft, or petty theft (committed at age 14 or older or stolen goods valued over $50)
    - Stealing property or knowingly receiving stolen property
    - Unlawful or illegal entry

- Unlawful use of long distance telephone lines or any electronic transmission method
- Use of telephone or any electronic transmission method to abuse, annoy, harass, threaten, or torment another
- Wrongful appropriation of a motor vehicle, joyriding, or driving without the owner's consent; if the intent was to permanently deprive the owner of the vehicle, treat as grand larceny or grand theft—auto (Category 2)

- Example Category 4 offenses

  - Abusive language under circumstances to provoke breach of peace
  - Altered identification when intent is to purchase alcoholic beverages
  - Check: $50 or less, insufficient funds, or worthless
  - Committing or creating nuisance
  - Curfew violation
  - Damaging road signs
  - Disorderly conduct, creating disturbance or boisterous conduct, disturbing the peace
  - Failure to appear, comply with judgment, or answer or disobey summons
  - Fare evasion (including failure to pay turnstile fees)
  - Fighting, participating in a brawl
  - Illegal betting or gambling: operating an illegal handbook, raffle, lottery, or punch board
  - Juvenile noncriminal misconduct: beyond parental control, incorrigible, runaway, truant, or wayward
  - Liquor or alcohol: unlawful possession or consumption in a public place
  - Littering or dumping refuse near highway or other prohibited place
  - Loitering
  - Purchase, possession, or consumption of alcoholic beverages by a minor
  - Shoplifting, larceny, petty larceny, theft, or petty theft (committed under age 14 and stolen goods valued at $50 or less)
  - Tobacco; unlawful possession or purchase
  - Trespass on property
  - Unlawful assembly
  - Vagrancy
  - Vandalism, defacing or injuring property
  - Violation of fireworks law
  - Violation of fish and game laws

- Example Category 5 offenses

  - Blocking or retarding traffic
  - Careless or reckless driving
  - Crossing the yellow line, drifting left of center
  - Disobeying traffic lights, signs, or signals
  - Driving on shoulder
  - Driving uninsured vehicle
  - Driving with blocked or impaired vision

- Driving with expired plates or without plates
- Driving with suspended or revoked license or without license
- Driving without license in possession
- Driving without registration or with improper registration
- Driving wrong way on a one-way street
- Failure to comply with an officer's direction
- Failure to display inspection sticker
- Failure to have vehicle under control
- Failure to keep right or in proper lane
- Failure to signal
- Failure to stop or yield to a pedestrian
- Failure to yield right of way
- Faulty equipment (defective exhaust, horn, lights, illegal window tint)
- Following too close
- Improper backing
- Improper blowing of horn
- Improper passing
- Improper turn
- Invalid or unofficial inspection sticker
- Leaving key in ignition
- License plates improperly or not displayed
- Operating overloaded vehicle
- Playing vehicle radio or stereo too loud (noise or sound pollution)
- Racing, drag racing, contest for speed
- Seatbelt violation
- Speeding
- Spinning wheels, improper start
- Zigzagging or weaving in traffic

Appendix B: Example of Integrity Testing and False Positives

Dalton and Metzger (1993) proposed that integrity tests that attempt to predict relatively rare or infrequent behaviors have a high potential to inaccurately classify a large number of people as prone to exhibit an infrequent behavior. For example, as Table B.1 shows, a test that is 70 percent accurate in its ability to classify individuals as having a behavior with a 5 percent base rate (i.e., a behavior exhibited by 5 percent of the population) may be expected to correctly categorize only 10.94 percent of test takers.

Notably, Dalton and Metzger assumed that the tests shown in Table B.1 are equally accurate in their ability to correctly classify someone as not having a characteristic (i.e., true negative) as they are in their ability to correctly classify someone as having the characteristic (i.e., true positive) . Others have also made this assumption (Martin, 1989). However, tests do not always (or often) demonstrate equivalent accuracy in establishing true positives and true negatives

Table B.1. Integrity Testing and False Positives

Test Accuracy[a]	Behavior Base Rate	Number Tested	Applicants with Behavior	Applicants Without Behavior	Number Correctly Identified as Having Behavior (true positives)	Number Incorrectly Identified as Having Behavior (false positives)	Proportion Correctly Identified as Having Behavior (%)
0.8	0.01	10,000	100	9,900	80	1,980	3.88
0.7	0.01	10,000	100	9,900	70	2,970	2.30
0.6	0.01	10,000	100	9,900	60	3,960	1.49
0.5	0.01	10,000	100	9,900	50	4,950	1.00
0.8	0.05	10,000	500	9,500	400	1,900	17.39
0.7	0.05	10,000	500	9,500	350	2,850	10.94
0.6	0.05	10,000	500	9,500	300	3,800	7.32
0.5	0.05	10,000	500	9,500	250	4,750	5.00
0.8	0.10	10,000	1,000	9,000	800	1,800	30.77
0.7	0.10	10,000	1,000	9,000	700	2,700	20.59
0.6	0.10	10,000	1,000	9,000	600	3,600	14.29
0.5	0.10	10,000	1,000	9,000	500	4,500	10.00
0.8	0.15	10,000	1,500	8,500	1,200	1,700	41.38
0.7	0.15	10,000	1,500	8,500	1,050	2,550	29.17
0.6	0.15	10,000	1,500	8,500	900	3,400	20.93
0.5	0.15	10,000	1,500	8,500	750	4,250	15.00

NOTE: Based on a model in Dalton and Metzger, 1993.
[a] Ability to correctly determine true positives and true negatives.

(see NRC, 2003). Table 3.1 addresses this and provides values based on the binomial equivariance model. However, Table B.1 provides an, arguably, more-intuitive description of the broad issue of misclassification.

Applying this example to the military specifically, previous research found that 9.9 percent to 11.6 percent of male Navy recruits reported perpetrating rape (Merrill, Thomsen, et al., 2001). The proportion of Air Force recruits who have previously perpetrated sexual assault may be much lower, as suggested by recent research demonstrating that sexual assault behaviors occur less frequently in the Air Force than in the Navy (Jaycox et al., 2015).[36] However, for illustrative purposes only, one may assume that approximately 10 percent of Air Force applicants may have perpetrated or be inclined to perpetrate sexual assault. This would suggest a behavior base rate of 10 percent among Air Force applicants. If one assumes that a measure for sexual assault can be developed that is 70 percent accurate, a test with this level of accuracy that is predicting a behavior with a base rate of 10 percent may be expected to correctly identify only 20.59 percent of test takers.

---

[36] Notably, previous research using nonmilitary samples has suggested that sexual assault may occur more frequently than reported (Abbey et al., 1996).

References

Abbey, Antonia, and Pam McAuslan, "A Longitudinal Examination of Male College Students' Perpetration of Sexual Assault," *Journal of Consulting and Clinical Psychology,* Vol. 72, No. 5, October 2004, pp. 747–756.

Abbey, Antonia, Pam McAuslan, and Lisa Thomson Ross, "Sexual Assault Perpetration by College Men: The Role of Alcohol, Misperception of Sexual Intent, and Sexual Beliefs and Experiences," *Journal of Social and Clinical Psychology,* Vol. 17, No. 2, June 1998, pp. 167–195.

Abbey, Antonia, Pam McAuslan, Tina Zawaki, A. Monique Clinton, and Philip O. Buck, "Attitudinal, Experiential, and Situational Predictors of Sexual Assault Perpetration," *Journal of Interpersonal Violence,* Vol. 16, No. 8, 2001, pp. 784-807.

Abbey, Antonia, Lisa Thomson Ross, Donna McDuffie, and Pam McAuslan, "Alcohol, Misperception, and Sexual Assault: How and Why Are They Linked?" in David M. Buss and Neil M. Malamuth, eds., *Sex, Power, Conflict: Evolutionary and Feminist Perspectives,* New York: Oxford University Press, 1996, pp. 138–161.

AETC—*See* Air Education and Training Command.

AFPC—*See* Air Force Personnel Center.

AFRS—*See* Air Force Recruiting Service.

Air Education and Training Command, *Identify and Qualify Recruit Candidates 09172009* [Business Process], 2008.

Air Force Instruction 36-2907, *Unfavorable Information File (UIF) Program*, November 26, 2014.

Air Force Instruction 36-6001, *Sexual Assault Prevention and Response (SAPR) Program*, October 14, 2010. As of June 12, 2014: http://www.afpc.af.mil/shared/media/document/AFD-130510-040.pdf

Air Force Pamphlet 36-2241, U.S. Air Force, *Professional Development Guide*, 40th anniv. ed., Washington, D.C.: Department of the Air Force, October 1, 2013. As of February 7, 2014: http://static.e-publishing.af.mil/production/1/af_a1/publication/afpam36-2241/afpam36-2241.pdf

Air Force Personnel Center, *Recruiting & Accession Waivers*, April 2010.

———, "Report Builder," web page, January 2015. As of January 22, 2015:
http://access.afpc.af.mil/vbinDMZ/broker.exe?_program=ideaspub.IDEAS_Step1.sas&_servi
ce=pZ1pub1&_debug=0

Air Force Policy Directive 36-60, *Sexual Assault Prevention and Response (SAPR) Program*,
2008. As of June 12, 2014:
http://www.sapr.mil/public/docs/policy/afpd36-60.pdf

Haygood, Angelo, *Welcome BMT Leaders*, briefing, Joint Base San Antonio-Randolph, Tex.: Air
Force Recruiting Service, 2013.

Air Force Recruiting Service Instruction 36-2001, *Recruiting Procedures for the Air Force*, Joint
Base San Antonio-Randolph, Tex.: Air Force Recruiting Service, 2012.

Alliger, George M., and Stephen A. Dwight, "A Meta-Analytic Investigation of the
Susceptibility of Integrity Tests to Faking and Coaching," *Educational and Psychological
Measurement,* Vol. 60, No. 1, February 2000, pp. 59–72.

Altemeyer, Bob, *The Authoritarian Specter,* Cambridge, Mass.: Harvard University Press, 1996.

Anderson, Linda A., and Susan C. Whitson, "Sexual Assault Education Programs: A Meta-
Analytic Examination of Their Effectiveness," *Psychology of Women Quarterly,* Vol. 29,
No. 4, December 2005, pp. 374–388.

Appelbaum, Steven H., Jennifer Cottin, and Remy Paré, and Barbara T. Shapiro, "Employee
Theft: From Behavioural Causation and Prevention to Managerial Detection and Remedies,"
Journal of American Academy of Business, Vol. 9, No. 2, September 2006, pp. 175–182.

Army Regulation 601-210, *Active and Reserve Components Enlistment Program*, March 2013.

Asch, Beth J., and Paul Heaton, *An Analysis of the Incidence of Recruiter Irregularities*, Santa
Monica, Calif.: RAND Corporation, TR-827-OSD, 2010. As of October 20, 2015:
http://www.rand.org/pubs/technical_reports/TR827.html

Ash, Philip, "Convicted Felon's Attitudes Towards Theft," *Criminal Justice and Behavior,*
Vol. 1, No. 1, March 1974, pp. 21–29.

Baker, Elina, and Anthony R. Beech, "Dissociation and Variability of Adult Attachment
Dimensions and Early Maladaptive Schemas in Sexual and Violent Offenders," *Journal of
Interpersonal Violence*, Vol. 19, No. 10, October 2004, pp. 1119–1136.

Barling, Julian, Kathryne E. Dupré, and E. Kevin Kelloway, "Predicting Workplace Aggression
and Violence," *Annual Review of Psychology,* Vol. 60, 2009, pp. 671–692.

Barrick, Murray R., and Michael K. Mount, "The Big Five Personality Dimensions and Job
Performance: A Meta-Analysis," *Personnel Psychology,* Vol. 44, No. 1, March 1991, pp. 1–
26.

Barron, Laura G., and Alan D. Ogle, "Individual Differences in Instructor Attitudes Underlying Maltreatment and Effective Mentoring," *Military Psychology,* Vol. 26, No. 5–6, September–November 2014, pp. 386–396.

Basile, Kathleen C., Sharon G. Smith, Matthew J. Breiding, Michele C. Black, and Reshma Mahendra, *Sexual Violence Surveillance: Uniform Definitions and Recommended Data Elements,* Atlanta, Ga.: Centers for Disease Control and Prevention, 2014.

Begany, Joseph J., and Michael A. Milburn, "Psychological Predictors of Sexual Harassment: Authoritarianism, Hostile Sexism, and Rape Myths," *Psychology of Men and Masculinity,* Vol. 3, No. 2, June 2002, pp. 119–126.

Bem, Sandra L. "The Measurement of Psychological Androgyny," *Journal of Clinical and Consulting Psychology*, Vol. 42, No. 2, April 1974, pp. 155–162.

Berry, Christopher M., and Paul R. Sackett, "Faking in Personnel Selection: Tradeoffs in Performance Versus Fairness Resulting from Two Cut-Score Strategies," *Personnel Psychology,* Vol. 62, No. 4, Winter 2009, pp. 835–863.

Berry, Christopher M., Paul R. Sackett, and Vanessa Tobares, "A Meta-Analysis of Conditional Reasoning Tests of Aggression," *Personnel Psychology,* Vol. 63, No. 2, Summer 2010, pp. 361–384.

Berry, Christopher M., Paul R. Sackett, and Shelly Wiemann, "A Review of Recent Developments in Integrity Test Research," *Personnel Psychology,* Vol. 60, No. 2, Summer 2007, pp. 271–301.

Bingham, Shereen G., and Brant R. Burleson., "The Development of a Sexual Harassment Proclivity Scale: Construct Validation and Relationship to Communication Competence," *Communication Quarterly,* Vol. 44, No. 3, June 1996, pp. 308–325.

Blau, Gary, and Lynne Andersson, "Testing a Measure of Instigated Workplace Incivility," *Journal of Occupational and Organizational Psychology,* Vol. 78, No. 4, December 2005, pp. 595–614.

Bohner, Gerd, and Norbert Schwartz, "The Threat of Rape: Its Psychological Impact on Nonvictimized Women," in David M. Buss and Neil M. Malamuth, eds., *Sex, Power, Conflict: Evolutionary and Feminist Perspectives,* New York: Oxford University Press, 1996, pp. 162–175.

Briere, John, and Neil M. Malamuth, "Self-Reported Likelihood of Sexually Aggressive Behavior: Attitudinal Versus Sexual Explanations," *Journal of Research in Personality,* Vol. 17, September 1983, pp. 315–323.

Brown, Reagan D., and Christopher M. Cothern, "Individual Differences in Faking Integrity Tests," *Psychological Reports,* Vol. 91, No. 3, December 2002, pp. 691–702.

Buck, Kelly R., and Michelle M. Neal, *Military Accession and Security Clearance Screening Impact on Early and Adverse Separation,* Monterey, Calif.: Defense Personnel Security Research Center, 2008.

Budd, John W., Richard D. Arvey, and Peggy Lawless, "Correlates and Consequences of Workplace Violence," *Journal of Occupational Health Psychology,* Vol. 1, No. 2, May 1996, pp. 197–210.

Buddin, Richard, *Analysis of Early Military Attrition Behavior,* Santa Monica, Calif.: RAND Corporation, R-3069-MIL, 1984. As of October 20, 2015: http://www.rand.org/pubs/reports/R3069.html

Burroughs, Susan M., and Lawrence R. James., "Advancing the Assessment of Dispositional Aggressiveness through Conditional Reasoning," in Suzy Fox and Paul E. Spector, eds., *Counterproductive Work Behavior: Investigations of Actors and Targets*, Washington, D.C.: American Psychological Association, 2005, pp. 127–150.

Buss, Arnold H., and Mark P. Perry, "The Aggression Questionnaire," *Journal of Personality and Social Psychology,* Vol. 63, No. 3, September 1992, pp. 452–459.

Butler, Matthew G., "The Valued Airman: Fostering Air Force Cultural Intolerance of Sexual Assault," Nellis Air Force Base, Nev.: 99th Air Base Wing, Air Combat Command, October 25, 2012. As of December 15, 2014: http://www.afpc.af.mil/shared/media/document/AFD-121205-041.pdf

Camara, Wayne J., and Dianne L. Schneider, "Integrity Tests: Facts and Unresolved Issues," *American Psychologist,* Vol. 49, No. 2, February 1994, pp. 112–119.

Cantor, James M., Ray Blanchard, Lori K. Robichaud, and Bruce K. Christensen, "Quantitative Reanalysis of Aggregate Data on IQ in Sexual Offenders," *Psychological Bulletin,* Vol. 131, No. 4, July 2005, pp. 555–568.

Capaldi, Deborah M., Thomas J. Dishion, Mike Stoolmiller, and Karen Yoerger, "Aggression Toward Female Partners by At-Risk Young Men: The Contribution of Male Adolescent Friendships," *Developmental Psychology,* Vol. 37, No. 1, January 2001, pp. 61–73.

Carless, Sally, A., "Person-Job Fit Versus Person-Organization Fit as Predictors of Organizational Attraction and Job Acceptance Intentions: A Longitudinal Study," *Journal of Occupational and Organization Psychology,* Vol. 78, No. 3, September 2005, pp. 411–429.

Carr, Joetta L., and Karen M. VanDeusen, "Risk Factors for Male Sexual Aggression on College Campuses," *Journal of Family Violence,* Vol. 19, No. 5, October 2004, pp. 279–289.

Chapman, Derek S., Krista L. Uggerslav, Sarah A. Carroll, Kelly A. Piasentin, and David A. Jones, "Applicant Attraction to Organization and Job Choice: A Meta-Analytic Review of the Correlates of Recruiting Outcomes," *Journal of Applied Psychology,* Vol. 90, No. 5, September 2005, pp. 928–944.

Christiansen, Neil D., Gary N. Burns, and George E. Montgomery, "Reconsidering Forced-Choice Items for Applicant Personality Assessment," *Human Performance,* Vol. 18, No. 3, 2005, pp. 267–307.

Civil Rights Act of 1964.

Civil Rights Act of 1991.

Cullen, Michael J., and Paul R. Sackett, "Integrity Testing in the Workplace," in J. C. Thomas and M. Hersen, eds., *Comprehensive Handbook of Psychological Assessment*, Vol. 4: *Industrial and Organizational Psychology,* Hoboken, N.J.: John Wiley & Sons, 2004, pp. 149–165.

Dalton, Dan R., and Michael B. Metzger, "'Integrity Testing' for Personnel Selection: An Unsparing Perspective," *Journal of Business Ethics,* Vol. 12, No. 2, February 1993, pp. 147–156.

Davis, Kristin, "Recruiter Pleads Guilty in Sexual Misconduct Trial," *Air Force Times*, June 2013, As of January 29, 2014:
http://www.airforcetimes.com/article/20130607/NEWS06/306070021/Recruiter-pleads-guilty-sexual-misconduct-trial

Day, Kristen, "Assault Prevention as Social Control: Women and Sexual Assault Prevention on Urban College Campuses," *Journal of Environment Psychology,* Vol. 15, No. 4, December 1995, pp. 261–281.

DD—*See* Directives Division.

De Keseredy, Walter S., and Katharine Kelly, "Sexual Abuse in Canadian University and College Dating Relationships: The Contribution of Male Peer Support," *Journal of Family Violence,* Vol. 10, No. 1, March 1995, pp. 41–53.

Department of Defense Instruction 1304.32, *Military Services Recruiting Related Reports*, March 26, 2013.

Dilchert, Stephan, Deniz S. Ones, Robert D. Davis, and Cary D. Rostow, "Cognitive Ability Predicts Objectively Measured Counterproductive Work Behaviors," *Journal of Applied Psychology,* Vol. 92, No. 3, May 2007, pp. 616–627.

Directives Division Form 2807-1, Report of Medical History, March 2015.

——— Form 2807-2, Accessions Medical Prescreen Report, March 2015.

——— Form 2808, Report of Medical Examination, October 2005.

—— Form 1966, Record of Military Processing, September 2014.

Douglas, Scott C., and Mark J. Martinko., "Exploring the Role of Individual Differences in the Prediction of Workplace Aggression," *Journal of Applied Psychology,* Vol. 86, No. 4, August 2001, pp. 547–559.

Drasgow, Fritz, Stephen Stark, Oleksandr S. Chernyshenko, Christoper D. Nye, and Charles L. Hulin, and Leonard A. White, *Development of the Tailored Adaptive Personality Assessment System to Support Army Selection and Classification Decisions,* Ft.. Belvoir, Va.: U.S. Army Research Institute for the Behavioral and Social Sciences, 2012.

Drieschner, Klaus, and Alfred Lange, "A Review of the Cognitive Factors in the Etiology of Rape: Theories, Empirical Studies, and Implications," *Clinical Psychology Review,* Vol. 19, No. 1, January 1999, pp. 57–77.

Driscoll, Marcy P., *Psychology of Learning for Instruction*, Boston: Allyn and Bacon, 2000.

Driskell, James E., Ruth P. Willis, and Carolyn Copper, "Effect of Overlearning on Retention," *Journal of Applied Psychology,* Vol. 77, No. 5, October 1992, pp. 615–622.

Duhart, Detis T., "Violence in the Workplace 1993–99," Washington, D.C.: Bureau of Justice Statistics, December 2001. As of July 30, 2014:
http://www.bjs.gov/content/pub/pdf/vw99.pdf

Earnest, David R., David G. Allen, and Ronald S. Landis, "Mechanism Linking Realistic Job Previews with Turnover: A Meta-Analytic Path Analysis," *Personnel Psychology,* Vol. 64, No. 4, Winter 2011, pp. 865–897.

Equal Employment Opportunity Commission, "Employment Tests and Selection Procedures," web page, September 23, 2010. As of January 23, 2015:
http://www.eeoc.gov/policy/docs/factemployment_procedures.html

Farris, Coreen, and Kimberly A. Hepner, *Targeting Alcohol Misuse: A Promising Strategy for Reducing Military Sexual Assault?,* Santa Monica, Calif.: RAND Corporation, RR-538-OSD, 2014. As of November 9, 2015:
http://www.rand.org/pubs/research_reports/RR538.html

Farris, Coreen, Lisa H. Jaycox, Terry L. Schell, Amy E. Street, Dean G. Kilpatrick, and Terri Tanielian, "Sexual Harassment and Gender Discrimination Findings: Active Component," in Andrew R. Morral, Kristie L. Gore, and Terry L. Schell, eds., *Sexual Assault and Sexual Harassment in the U.S. Military*, Vol. 2: *Estimates for Department of Defense Service Members from the 2014 RAND Military Workplace Study,* Santa Monica, Calif.: RAND Corporation, RR-870/2-OSD, 2015, pp. 31–54. As of October 20, 2015:
http://www.rand.org/pubs/research_reports/RR870z2.html

Faust, Quentin Collin, "Integrity Tests: Do They Have Any Integrity, *Cornell Journal of Law and Policy,* Vol. 6, No. 1, 1996, pp. 211–232.

Fernandez, Yolanda M., and W. L. Marshall, "Victim Empathy, Social Self-Esteem, and Psychopathy in Rapists," *Sexual Abuse: A Journal of Research and Treatment,* Vol. 15, No. 1, January 2003, pp. 11–26.

Fletcher, Tony A., Samuel Jan Brakel, and James L. Cavanaugh., "Violence in the Workplace: New Perspectives in Forensic Mental Health Services in the USA," *British Journal of Psychiatry,* Vol. 176, No. 4, April 2000, pp. 339–344.

Foldes, Hannah J., Emily E. Duehr, and Deniz S. Ones, "Group Differences in Personality: Meta-Analyses Comparing Five U.S. Racial Groups," *Personnel Psychology,* Vol. 61, No. 3, Autumn 2008, pp. 579–616.

Fortmann, Kristen, Curt Leslie, and Michael Cunningham, "Cross-Cultural Comparisons of the Reid Integrity Scale in Latin America and South Africa," *International Journal of Selection and Assessment,* Vol. 10, Nos. 1–2, March 2002, pp. 98–108.

Garb, Howard N., Aaron Wirick, and James M. Wood, "The Lackland Behavioral Questionnaire (LBQ) and the Prediction of Attrition, Mental Health, Criminal, and Personnel Reliability Program (PRP) Outcomes," Lackland Air Force Base, Tex.: Psychology Research Service 559th Medical Operations Squadron, 2012.

Garb, Howard N., James M. Wood, Kristin Schneider, Monty Baker, and Wendy Travis, "Suitability Screening During Basic Military Training," *Military Psychology,* Vol. 25, No. 1, January 2013, pp. 82–91.

Genetic Information Nondiscrimination Act of 2008.

Glick, Peter, and Susan T. Fiske, "The Ambivalent Sexism Inventory: Differentiating Hostile and Benevolent Sexism," *Journal of Personality and Social Psychology,* Vol. 70, No. 3, March 1996, pp. 491–512.

Goodell, Maia, "Physical-Strength Rationales for De Jure Exclusion of Women from Military Combat Positions," *Seattle University Law Review,* Vol. 34, No. 1, 2010, pp. 17–50.

Gough, H. G., *Manual for the Personnel Reaction Blank,* Palo Alto, Calif.: Consulting Psychologists Press, 1972.

Greathouse, Sarah Michal, Jessica Saunders, Miriam Matthews, Kirsten M. Keller, and Laura L. Miller, *A Review of the Literature on Sexual Assault Perpetrator Characteristics and Behaviors,* Santa Monica, Calif.: RAND Corporation, RR-1082-AF, 2015. As of January 8, 2016:
http://www.rand.org/pubs/research_reports/RR1082.html

Greenberg, Jerald, and Bradley J. Algae., "Aggressive Reactions to Workplace Injustice," in Ricky W. Griffin, Anne O'Leary-Kelly, and Judith M. Collins, eds., *Dysfunctional Behavior in Organizations: Violent and Deviant Behavior,* Stamford, Conn.: JAI Press, 1998.

Grubb, Paula L., Rashaun L. Roberts, Namoi G. Swanson, Jennifer L. Burnfield, and Jennifer H. Childress, "Organizational Factors and Psychological Aggression: Results from a Nationally Representative Sample of US Companies," in Vaughan Bowie, Bonnie S. Fisher, and Cary L. Cooper, eds., *Workplace Violence: Issues, Trends, Strategies,* 2005, pp. 37–59.

Guastello, Stephen J., and Mark L. Rieke, "A Review and Critique of Honesty Test Research," *Behavioral Sciences and Law*, Vol. 9, No. 4, Autumn 1991, pp. 501–523.

Gutman, Arthur, Laura L. Koppes, and Stephen Vodanovich, *EEO Law and Personnel Practices*, 3rd ed., New York: Taylor and Francis, 2011.

Hall, Gordon C. Nagayama, "Prediction of Sexual Aggression," *Clinical Psychology Review,* Vol. 10, No. 2, 1990, pp. 229–245.

Hall, Gordon C. Nagayama, Stanley Sue, David S. Narang, and Roy S. Lilly, "Culture-Specific Models of Men's Sexual Aggression: Intra- and Interpersonal Determinants," *Cultural Diversity and Ethnic Minority Psychology,* Vol. 6, No. 3, August 2000, pp. 252–267.

Hammock, Georgina S., and Deborah R. Richardson, "Predictors of Aggressive Behavior," *Aggressive Behavior,* Vol. 18, No. 3, 1992, pp. 219–229.

Haygood, Angelo, Bullet Background Paper on AFRS Waiver Process, Air Force Recruiting Service, undated.

Headquarters Air Force Recruiting Service, Recruiting Service Operations, "Deter, Detect, Dissuade and Accountability (D3A)," procedural guidance message, September 23, 2013.

Heggestad, Eric D., Morgan Morrison, Charlie L. Reeve, and Rodney A. McCloy, "Forced-Choice Assessments of Personality for Selection: Evaluating Issues of Normative Assessment and Faking Resistance," *Journal of Applied Psychology,* Vol. 91, No. 1, January 2006, pp. 9–24.

Hershcovis, M. Sandy, Nick Turner, Julian Barling, Kara A. Arnold, Kathryn E. Dupre, Michelle Inness, Manon Mireille LeBlanc, and Niro Sivanathan., "Predicting Workplace Aggression: A Meta-Analysis," *Journal of Applied Psychology,* Vol. 92, No. 1, January 2007, pp. 228–238.

Hogan, Robert, and Joyce Hogan, *Hogan Personality Inventory Manual*, Tulsa, Okla.: Hogan Assessment Systems, 2007.

Hollwitz, John C., and Donna R. Pawlowski, "The Development of a Structured Ethical Integrity Interview for Pre-Employment Screening," *The Journal of Business Communication,* Vol. 34, No. 2, April 1997, pp. 203–219.

Hough, Leaetta M., Newell K. Eaton, Marvin D. Dunnette, John D. Kemp, and Rodney A. McCloy, "Criterion-Related Validities of Personality Constructs and the Effect of Response Distortion on Those Validities," *Journal of Applied Psychology,* Vol. 75, No. 5, October 1990, pp. 581–595.

Hough, Leaetta M., and Frederick L. Oswald., "Personnel Selection: Looking Toward the Future—Remembering the Past," *Annual Review of Psychology,* Vol. 51, 2000, pp. 631–664.

Jackson, Douglas N., Victor R. Wroblewski, and Michael C. Aston, "The Impact of Faking on Employment Tests: Does Forced Choice Offer a Solution?" *Human Performance,* Vol. 13, No. 4, 2000, pp. 371–388.

Jaycox, Lisa H., Terry L. Schell, Andrew R. Morral, Amy Street, Coreen Farris, Dean Kilpatrick, and Terri Tanielian, "Sexual Assault Findings: Active Component," in Andrew R. Morral, Kristie L. Gore, and Terry L. Schell, eds., *Sexual Assault and Sexual Harassment in the U.S. Military*, Vol. 2: *Estimates for Department of Defense Service Members from the 2014 RAND Military Workplace Study,* Santa Monica, Calif.: RAND Corporation, RR-870/2-OSD, 2015, pp. 9–30. As of October 20, 2015:
http://www.rand.org/pubs/research_reports/RR870z2.html

Jewkes, Rachel, Purna Sen, and Claudia Garcia-Moreno, "Sexual Violence," in Etienne G. Kruc, Linda L. Dahlberg, James A. Mercy, Anthony B. Zwi, and Rafael Lozano, eds., *World Report on Violence and Health,* Geneva: World Health Organization, 2002, pp. 149–181.

John, Oliver P. and Veronica Benet-Martínez, "Measurement, Scale Construction, and Reliability," in Harry T. Reis and Charles M. Judd, eds., *Handbook of Research Methods in Social and Personality Psychology*, New York: Cambridge University Press, 2000, pp. 339–369.

John, Oliver P., and Christopher J. Soto, "The Importance of Being Valid: Reliability and the Process of Construct Validation," in Richard W. Robins, R. Chris Fraley, and Robert F. Krueger, eds., *Handbook of Research Methods in Personality Psychology*, 2009, pp. 461–494.

John, Oliver P., and Sanjay Srivastava, "The Big Five Trait Taxonomy: History, Measurement, and Theoretical Perspectives," in Lawrence A. Pervin and Oliver P. John, eds., *Handbook of Personality: Theory and Research,* 2nd ed., 1999, pp. 102–137.

Judge, Timothy A., Joseph J. Martocchio, and Carl J. Thoresen, "Five-Factor Model of Personality and Employee Absence," *Journal of Applied Psychology,* Vol. 82, No. 5, October 1997, pp. 745–755.

Kent, R., and M. Martinko, "The Development and Evaluation of a Scale to Measure Organizational Attributional Style," in Mark Martinko, ed., *Attribution Theory: An Organizational Perspective,* 1995, Delray Beach, Fla.: St. Lucie Press, pp. 53–75.

Kirkpatrick, Donald. "Seven Keys to Unlock the Four Levels of Evaluation," *Performance Improvement,* Vol. 45, No. 7, August 2006, pp. 5–8.

Kobbs, Steven W., and Richard D. Arvey, "Distinguishing Deviant and Non-Deviant Nurses Using the Personnel Reaction Blank," *Journal of Business and Psychology,* Vol. 8, No. 2, December 1993, pp. 255–264.

Koss, Mary P., Antonia Abbey, Rebecca Campbell, Sarah Cook, Jeanette Norris, Maria Testa, Sarah Ullman, Carolyn West, and Jacquelyn White, "The Sexual Experiences Long Form Perpetration (SES-LFP)," tool, Tucson, Ariz.: University of Arizona, 2006.

Koss, Mary P., and Cheryl J. Oros, "Sexual Experiences Survey: A Research Instrument Investigating Sexual Aggression and Victimization," *Journal of Consulting and Clinical Psychology,* Vol. 50, No. 3, June 1982, pp. 455–457.

Latham, Larry L., and Richard Perlow, "The Relationship of Client-Directed Aggressive and Nonclient-Directed Aggressive Work Behavior with Self Control," *Journal of Applied Social Psychology,* Vol. 26, No. 12, June 1996, pp. 1027–1041.

LeBreton, James M., Cheryl D. Barksdale, Jennifer Robin, and Lawrence R. James, "Measurements Issues Associated with Conditional Reasoning Tests: Indirect Measurement and Test Faking," *Journal of Applied Psychology,* Vol. 92, No. 1, January 2007, pp. 1–16.

Lee, Robin Wilbourn, Michele E. Caruso, Shelley E. Goins, and Jennifer P. Southerland, "Addressing Sexual Assault on College Campuses: Guidelines for a Prevention/Awareness Week," *Journal of College Counseling,* Vol. 6, No. 1, Spring 2003, pp. 14–24.

Lieber, Lynn, "Workplace Violence—What Can Employers Do to Prevent It?" *Employee Relations Today*, Vol. 34, No. 3, Autumn 2007, pp. 91–100.

Loh, Catherine, Christine A. Gidycz, Tracy R. Lobo, and Rohini Luthra, "A Prospective Analysis of Sexual Assault Perpetration: Risk Factors Related to Perpetrator Characteristics," *Journal of Interpersonal Violence*, Vol. 20, No. 10, October 2005, pp. 1325–1348.

MacCann, Carolyn, Matthias Ziegler, and Richard Roberts, "Faking in Personality Assessment: Reflections and Recommendations," in Matthias Ziegler, Carolyn MacCann, and Richard D. Roberts, eds*., New Perspectives on Faking in Personality Assessment*, New York: Oxford University Press, 2011, pp. 309–329.

Malamuth, Neil M., "Rape Proclivity Among Males," *Journal of Social Issues,* Vol. 37, No. 4, Fall 1981, pp. 138–157.

————, "Predictors of Naturalistic Sexual Aggression," *Journal of Personality and Social Psychology,* Vol. 50, No. 5, May 1986, pp. 953–962.

————, "A Mutidimensional Approach to Sexual Aggression: Combining Measures of Past Behavior and Present Likelihood," in Robert A. Prentky and Vernon L. Quinsey, eds., *Human Sexual Aggression: Current Perspectives,* Annals of the New York Academy of Sciences, Vol. 528, 1988, pp. 123–132.

————, "The Confluence Model of Sexual Aggression: Feminist and Evolutionary Perspectives," in David M. Buss and Neil M. Malamuth, eds., *Sex, Power, Conflict: Evolutionary and Feminist Perspectives,* New York: Oxford University Press, 1996, pp. 269–295.

Malamuth, Neil M., Daniel Linz, Christopher L. Heavey, Gordon Barnes, and Michele Acker, "Using the Confluence Model of Sexual Aggression to Predict Men's Conflict with Women: A 10-Year Follow-Up Study," *Journal of Personality and Social Psychology,* Vol. 69, No. 2, 1995, pp. 353–369.

Martin, Scott L., "Honesty Testing: Estimating and Reducing the False Positive Rate," *Journal of Business and Psychology,* Vol. 3, No. 3, Spring 1989, pp. 255–267.

Martinko, Mark J., Michal J. Gundlach, and Scott C. Douglas, "Toward an Integrative Theory of Counterproductive Workplace Behavior: A Causal Reasoning Perspective," *International Journal of Selection and Assessment,* Vol. 10, Nos. 1–2, March–June 2002, pp. 36–50.

Masser, Barbara, G. Tendayi Viki, and Clair Power, "Hostile Sexism and Rape Proclivity Amongst Men," *Sex Roles,* Vol. 54, No. 7–8, April 2006, pp. 565–574.

Merrill, Lex L., Carol E. Newell, Joel S. Milner, Linda K. Hervig, and Steven R. Gold, *Prevalence of Premilitary Adult Sexual Victimization and Aggression in a Navy Basic Trainee Sample,* San Diego, Calif.: Naval Health Research Center, 1997.

Merrill, Lex L., Cynthia J. Thomsen, Steven R. Gold, and Joel S. Milner, "Childhood Abuse and Premilitary Sexual Assault in Male Navy Recruits," *Journal of Consulting and Clinical Psychology,* Vol. 69, No. 2, May 2001, pp. 252–261.

Metzger, Michael B., and Dan R. Dalton, "'Just Say No' to Integrity Testing," *University of Florida Journal of Law and Public Policy,* Vol. 4, No. 9, 1991, pp. 10–38.

McHenry, Jeffrey J., Leaetta M. Hough, Jody L. Toquam, Mary Ann Hanson, and Steven Ashworth, "Project A Validity Results: The Relationship Between Predictor and Criterion Domains," *Personnel Psychology,* Vol. 43, No. 2, June 1990, pp. 335–354.

Morgeson, Frederick P., Michael A. Campion, Robert L. Doyle, John R. Hollenbeck, Kevin Murphy, and Neal Schmitt, "Reconsidering the Use of Personality Tests in Personnel Selection Contexts," *Personnel Psychology,* Vol. 60, No. 2007, pp. 683–729.

Morral, Andrew R., Kristie L. Gore, and Terry L. Schell, eds., *Sexual Assault and Sexual Harassment in the U.S. Military*, Vol. 1: *Design of the 2014 RAND Military Workplace Study,* Santa Monica, Calif.: RAND Corporation, RR-870/1-OSD, 2014. As of October 20, 2015:
http://www.rand.org/pubs/research_reports/RR870z1.html

———, *Sexual Assault and Sexual Harassment in the U.S. Military,* Vol. 2: *Estimates for Department of Defense Service Members from the 2014 RAND Military Workplace Study*, Santa Monica, Calif.: RAND Corporation, RR-870/2-OSD, 2015. As of November 17, 2015:
http://www.rand.org/pubs/research_reports/RR870z2.html

Mumford, Michael D., Mary Shane Connelly, Whitney B. Helton, Jill M. Strange, and Holly K. Osburn, "On the Construct Validity of Integrity Tests: Individual and Situational Factors as Predictors of Test Performance," *International Journal of Selection and Assessment,* Vol. 9, No. 3, September 2001, pp. 240–257.

Murphy, Kevin R., "Detecting Infrequent Deception," *Journal of Applied Psychology,* Vol. 72, No. 4, November 1987, pp. 611–614.

National Research Council, *The Polygraph and Lie Detection,* Washington, D.C.: National Academies of Press, 2003.

Neuman, Joel H., and Robert A. Baron., "Workplace Violence and Workplace Aggression: Evidence Concerning Specific Form, Potential Causes, and Preferred Targets," *Journal of Management,* Vol. 24, No. 3, June 1998, pp. 391–419.

Niebuhr, David W., Marlene E. Gubata, Alexis A. Oetting, Natalya S. Weber, Xiaoshu Feng, and David N. Cowan, "Personality Assessment Questionnaire as a Pre-Accession Risk of Mental Disorders and Early Attrition in U.S. Army Recruits," *Psychological Services*, Vol. 10, No. 4, November 2013, pp. 378–385.

NRC—*See* National Research Council.

Nye, Christopher D., Fritz Drasgow, Oleksandr S. Chernyshenko, Stephen Stark, U. Christean Kubisiak, Leonard A. White, and Irwin Jose, *Assessing the Tailored Adaptive Personality Assessment System (TAPAS) as an MOS Qualification Instrument,* Ft.. Belvoir, Va.: U.S. Army Research Institute for the Behavioral and Social Sciences, 2012.

Occupational Safety and Health Administration, "Workplace Violence," fact sheet, Washington, D.C., 2002. Last retrieved on July 30, 2014 from
https://www.osha.gov/OshDoc/data_General_Facts/factsheet-workplace-violence.pdf

Office of the Deputy Assistant Secretary of Defense, *2012 Demographics: Profile of the Military Community,* Washington, D.C., 2013.

Office of Technology Assessment, *The Use of Integrity Tests for Pre-Employment Screening,* OTA-SET-442, Washington, D.C.: U.S. Government Printing Office, September 1990.

Oken, Carole, and Beth J. Asch, *Encouraging Recruiter Achievement: A Recent History of Military Recruiter Incentive Programs,* Santa Monica, Calif.: RAND Corporation, MR-845-OSD/A, 1997. As of October 20, 2015:
http://www.rand.org/pubs/monograph_reports/MR845.html

Ones, Deniz S., *Establishing the Construct Validity for Integrity Tests,* dissertation, Iowa City: University of Iowa, 1993.

Ones, Deniz S., and Neil Anderson, "Gender and Ethnic Group Difference on Personality Scales in Selection: Some British Data," *Journal of Occupational and Organizational Psychology,* Vol. 75, No. 3, September 2002, pp. 255–276.

Ones, Deniz S., Stephan Dilchert, Chockalingam Viswesvaran, and Timothy Judge, "In Support of Personality Assessment in Organizational Settings," *Personnel Psychology,* Vol. 60, No. 4, Winter 2007, pp. 995–1027.

Ones, Deniz S., and Chockalingam Viswesvaran, "Gender, Age, and Race Difference on Overt Integrity Tests: Results Across Four Large-Scale Job Applicant Data Sets," *Journal of Applied Psychology,* Vol. 83, No. 1, January 1998, pp. 35–42.

———, "Integrity Tests and Other Criterion-Focused Occupational Personality Scales (COPS) Used in Personnel Selection," *International Journal of Selection and Assessment,* Vol. 9, Nos. 1–2, March 2001, pp. 31–39.

Ones, Deniz S., Chockalingam Viswesvaran, and Frank L. Schmidt, "Comprehensive Meta-Analysis of Integrity Test Validities: Findings and Implications for Personnel Selection and Theories of Job Performance," *Journal of Applied Psychology,* Vol. 78, No. 4, July 1993, pp. 679–703.

OTA—*See* Office of Technology Assessment.

Paajanen, George E., Timothy L. Hansen, Richard A. McLellan, *Employment Inventory Research,* 1st ed., Minneapolis, Minn.: Technology Based Solutions, 1999.

Pina, Afroditi, Theresa A. Gannon, and Benjamin Saunders, "An Overview of the Literature on Sexual Harassment: Perpetrator, Theory, and Treatment Issues," *Aggression and Violent Behavior,* Vol. 14, No. 2, March–April 2009, pp. 126–138.

Pryor, John B., "Sexual Harassment Proclivities in Men," *Sex Roles,* Vol. 17, No. 5, September 1987, pp. 269–290

Ree, Malcolm James, James A. Earles, and Mark S. Teachout, "Predicting Job Performance: Not Much More than *g,*" *Journal of Applied Psychology,* Vol. 79, No. 4, July 1994, pp. 518–524.

Rehabilitation Act of 1973.

Roper v. Dep't of Army, 832 F.2d 247, 248 [2d Cir. 1987].

Rose, Mark R., Gregory G. Manley, and Johnny J. Weissmuller, *Development of Two- and Three-Factor Classification Models for Air Force Battlefield Airmen (BA) and Related AFSs*, Randolph AFB, Tex.: Air Force Personnel Center, Strategic Research and Assessment Branch, 2013.

Roszkowski, Michael J., and Scott Spreat, "Issues to Consider When Evaluating 'Tests,'" in J.E. Grable et al. (eds.), *Financial Planning and Counseling Scales,* 2011, pp. 13-31.

Roth, Philip L., Craig A. Bevier, Philip Bobko, Fred S. Switzer III, and Peggy Tyler, "Ethnic Group Differences in Cognitive Ability in Employment and Educational Setting: A Meta-Analysis," *Personnel Psychology,* Vol. 54, No. 2, June 2001, pp. 297–330.

Rothman, Emily, and Jay Silverman, "The Effect of a College Sexual Assault Prevention Program on First-year Students' Victimization Rates," Journal of American College Health, Vol. 55, No. 5, March–April 2007, pp. 283–290.

Ryan, Ann Marie, and Paul R. Sackett, "Pre-Employment Honesty Testing: Fakability, Reactions of Test Takers, and Company Image," *Journal of Business and Psychology,* Vol. 1, No. 3, March 1987, pp. 248–256.

Saad, Syed, Gary Carter, Mark Rothenberg, and Enid Israelson, *Testing and Assessments: An Employer's Guide to Good Practices,* Washington, D.C.: U.S. Department of Labor Employment and Training Administration, 1999.

Sackett, Paul R., Laura R. Burris, and Christine Callahan., "Integrity Testing for Personnel Selection: An Update," *Personnel Psychology,* Vol. 42, No. 3, September 1989, pp. 491–529.

Sackett, Paul R., and Michael M. Harris, "Honesty Testing for Personnel Selection: A Review and Critique," *Personnel Psychology,* Vol. 37, No. 2, June 1984, pp. 221–245.

Sackett, Paul R., and James E. Wanek, "New Developments in the Use of Measures of Honesty, Integrity , Conscientiousness, Dependability, Trustworthiness, and Reliability for Personnel Selection," *Personnel Psychology,* Vol. 49, No. 4, December 1996, pp. 787–829.

Sackett, Paul R., and Steffanie L. Wilk, "Within-Group Norming and Other Forms of Score Adjustment in Preemployment Testing," *American Psychologist,* Vol. 49, No. 11, November 1994, pp. 929–954.

Sarchione, Charles, Michael J. Cuttler, Paul M. Muchinsky, and Rosemery O. Nelson-Gray, "Prediction of Dysfunctional Job Behaviors Among Law Enforcement Officers," *Journal of Applied Psychology,* Vol. 83, No. 6, December 1998, pp. 904–912.

Saxe, Leonard, Denise Dougherty, and Theodore Cross, "The Validity of Polygraph Testing: Scientific Analyses and Public Controversy," *American Psychologist*, Vol. 40, No. 3, February 1985, pp. 355–366.

Schmidt, Frank L., and John E. Hunter, "The Validity and Utility of Selection Methods in Personnel Psychology: Practical and Theoretical Implications of 85 Years of Research Findings," *Psychological Bulleting,* Vol. 124, No. 2, September 1998, pp. 262–274.

Schmidt, Frank L., Chockalingam Viswesvaran, and Deniz S. Ones, "Validity of Integrity Tests for Predicting Drug and Alcohol Abuse: A Meta-Analysis," NIDA Research Monograph, 1997, pp. 69–95.

Schneider, Beth E., "Put Up and Shut Up: Workplace Sexual Assaults," *Gender & Society,* Vol. 5, No. 4, December 1991, pp. 533–548.

SF—*See* Standard Form.

Spielberger, Charles D., *State-Trait Anger Expression Inventory-2,* Odessa, Fla.: Psychological Publications, Inc., 1999.

Spitzberg, Brian H., "An Analysis of Empirical Estimates of Sexual Aggression Victimization and Perpetration," *Violence and Victims,* Vol. 14, No. 3, February 1999, pp. 241–260.

Stabile, Susan J., "The Use of Personality Tests as a Hiring Tool: Is the Benefit Worth the Cost?" *University of Pennsylvania Journal of Labor and Employment Law,* Vol. 4, No. 2, Winter 2002, pp. 279–313.

Standard Form 86, Questionnaire for National Security Positions, December 2010.

Stark, Stephen, Oleksandr S. Chernyshenko, Fritz Drasgow, and Leonard A. White, "Adaptive Testing with Multidimensional Pairwise Preference Items: Improving the Efficiency of Personality and Other Noncognitive Assessments," *Organizational Research Methods*, May 10, 2012, pp. 1–25.

Stark, Stephen, Oleksandr S. Chernyshenko, Fritz Drasgow, Christopher D. Nye, Leonard A. White, Tonia Heffner, and William L. Farmer, "From ABLE to TAPAS: A New Generation of Personality Tests to Support Military Selection and Classification Decisions," *Military Psychology*, Vol. 26, No. 3, May 2014, pp. 153–164.

Steinhaus, Stephen D., and Brian K. Waters, "Biodata and the Application of a Psychometric Perspective," *Military Psychology,* Vol. 3, No. 1, 1991, pp. 1–23.

Stuckless, Noreen, and Richard Goranson, "The Vengeance Scale: Development of a Measure of Attitudes Toward Revenge," *Journal of Social Behavior & Personality,* Vol. 7, No. 1, January 1992, pp. 25–42.

Swartout, Kevin M., and Jacquelyn W. White, "The Relationship Between Drug Use and Sexual Aggression in Men Across Time," *Journal of Interpersonal Violence,* Vol. 25, No. 9, 2010, pp. 1716–1735.

Swets, John A., Robyn M. Dawes, and John Monahan, "Better Decisions Through Science," *Scientific American,* 2000, pp. 82–87.

Tharp, Andra Teten, Sarah DeGue, Linda Anne Valle, Kathryn A. Brookmeyer, Greta M. Massetti, and Jennifer L. Matajasko, "A Systematic Qualitative Review of Risk and Protective Factors for Sexual Violence Perpetration," *Trauma, Violence, and Abuse,* Vol. 14, No. 2, April 2012, pp. 133–167.

Thompson, Martie P., Mary P. Koss, J. B. Kingree, Jennifer Goree, and John Rice, "A Prospective Mediational Model of Sexual Aggression Among College Men," *Journal of Interpersonal Violence*, Vol. 26, No. 13, September 2011, pp. 2716–2734.

Trent, Thomas, and Mary A. Quenette, *Armed Services Applicant Profile (ASAP): Development and Validation of Operational Forms,* San Diego, Calif.: Navy Personnel Research and Development Center, 1992.

U.S. Air Force, "Air Force Life," online FAQ, U.S. Air Force website, 2014. As of January 30, 2014:
http://www.airforce.com/contact-us/faq/

U.S. Code, Title 10, Section 502, Enlistment Oath: Who May Administer.

USMEPCOM—*See* U.S. U.S. Military Entry Processing Command.

U.S. Military Entry Processing Command Form 40-1-15-1-E, Medical History Provider Interview, undated.

——— Form 601-23-5-R-E, Introductory Preaccession Interview, October 1, 1999.

Van Iddekinge, Chad H., Philip L. Roth, Patrick H. Raymark, and Heather N. Odle-Dusseau, "The Criterion-Related Validity of Integrity Tests: An Updated Meta-Analysis," *Journal of Applied Psychology,* Vol. 97, No. 3, May 2012, pp. 499–530.

Vasilopoulos, Nicholas, Jeffrey M. Cucina, Natalia D. Dyomina, Courtney L. Morewitz, and Richard R. Reilly, "Forced-Choice Personality Tests: A Measure of Personality and Cognitive Ability?" *Human Performance,* Vol. 19, No. 3, 2006, pp. 175–199.

Wanek, James E., "Integrity and Honesty Testing: What Do We Know? How Do We Use It?" *International Journal of Selection and Assessment*, Vol. 7, No. 4. December 1999, pp. 183–195.

Welsh, Mark A., "Update on Basic Military Training Sexual Misconduct," statement before the House Armed Services Committee, January 23, 2013. As of June 12, 2014:

http://docs.house.gov/meetings/AS/AS00/20130123/100231/HHRG-113-AS00-Wstate-RiceG-20130123.pdf

Woehr, David J., Winfred Arthur, and Melinda L. Fehrmann, "An Empirical Comparison of Cutoff Score Methods for Content-Related and Criterion-Related Validity Settings," *Educational and Psychological Measurement,* Vol. 51, No. 4, Winter 1991, pp. 1029–1039.

Zawacki, Tina, Antonia Abbey, Philip O. Buck, Pamela McAuslan, and A. Monique Clinton-Sherrod, "Perpetrators of Alcohol-Involved Sexual Assaults: How Do They Differ from Other Sexual Assault Perpetrators and Nonperpetrators?" *Aggressive Behavior*, Vol. 29, No. 4, August 2003, pp. 366–380.

Zinzow, Heidi M., and Martie Thompson, "A Longitudinal Study of Risk Factors for Repeated Sexual Coercion and Assault in U.S. College Men," *Archives of Sexual Behavior*, Vol. 44, No. 1, January 2015, pp. 1–10.